Mantra and the Goddess

A Poetic Interpretation of the Sri Lalita Sahasranama

First published by O-Books, 2010
O Books is an imprint of John Hunt Publishing Ltd., The Bothy, Deershot Lodge, Park Lane, Ropley, Hants, SO24 0BE, UK
office1@o-books.net
www.o-books.com

For distributor details and how to order please visit the 'Ordering' section on our website.

ISBN: 978 1 84694 313 3

A CIP catalogue record for this book is available from the British Library.

Design: Stuart Davies

Printed in the UK by CPI Antony Rowe
Printed in the USA by Offset Paperback Mfrs, Inc

The Transindic Transliterator Gara fonts used to create this work are available from www.linguistsoftware.com/tintu.htm (Phone1.425.775.1130).

The author's proceeds from this book will be donated to Lalitamba Mandiram.

We operate a distinctive and ethical publishing philosophy in all areas of its business, from its global network of authors to production and worldwide distribution.

Mantra and the Goddess

A Poetic Interpretation of the Sri Lalita Sahasranama

Swamini Sri Lalitambika Devi

BOOKS

Winchester, UK
Washington, USA

CONTENTS

PART IV: Transliteration for Chanting

PART V: Epilogue

Dedicated to Marshall,
who spent the last thirteen days of his life with me,
during which time I cared for him
and worked on the revisions of this book.

PREFACE

THE GODDESS has been idealized by various cultures throughout history and probably will be so for eternity. She is sometimes depicted as a fierce and powerful warrior. The demon-slayer. The destroyer of ego. At the same time, She is gentle, generous, and unconditionally loving. She is the ultimate sex symbol to some, yet She may be perfectly chaste. It felt important to write an interpretation that reflected an internal experience of Her. Perhaps it is a form of Self-inquiry, an exploration of the question, "Who am I?"

The Goddess is one way to experience the presence that is both immanent and transcendent. This presence is beyond name and form. In truth, there are no words to describe it.

These writings are not a direct or literal translation of the *Sri Lalita Sahasranama*, nor are they meant to be. There are already a number of excellent literal translations available. This version is an interpretation of the Goddess. It seemed important that She be accessible to seekers from diverse cultural backgrounds. Some of the myths included have also been adapted as universal allegory. Please forgive any errors or words with which you do not agree.

In writing this book, I was inspired by the commentary of Bhaskararaya, Swami Tapasyananda, and T. K. Narayana Menon. I am also thankful for the depth and breadth of the Sanskrit dictionary by M. Monier-Williams, and the easeful brevity of that by Vasudeo Govind Apte. Both of these dictionaries were gifts from friends to whom I am grateful.

This book is an offering. I offer *pranams* to the *guru* for revealing our potential to be far greater than anything we could imagine. Many thanks to Gabriella Contestabile, Carol Emshwiller, Barbara Fleck-Paladino, Ada Nicolescu, Margaret Sweeny, Maria Tammik, and Gay Terry, for their insight and curiosity. I offer special thanks to Kathy Casey for her eagle eyes, her professional opinions, and just for being there. I am deeply grateful to John Hunt and the team at O Books: Trevor Greenfield, Nick Welch, Marie Crane, and Stuart Davies, for their work with the book, and to Joan Schweighardt for bringing it to their attention. I bow down to my family, all of whom helped me to mature emotionally and to grow spiritually. I love you. There are beloved teachers, students, and friends who are not named here but to whom I offer all that I can be, in love and gratitude. And the book is especially for you. The reader. The seeker.

When I was in India, my teacher used to say, "Don't worry. There is no limit to what you can do. There is no limit where *guru* or God is concerned."

I pass that on to you. There is no limit to what you can do, to who you can be, and to who you already are. Each of us is a great saint, and at the same time, nobody at all. Live in truth. Let yourself be vulnerable enough to merge with the heart, and so with all beings. Trust enough to go all the way with the One.

—*Swamini Sri Lalitambika Devi*

PART I:

A Gentle Turn of Mind

CHAPTER 1

The Power of Mantra

WHEN I WAS four years old, my father arranged for a meditation teacher to visit our summer rental and initiate me with a *mantra*. At the time, my father had been meditating himself for only two years. Still, sitting had become an extended daily practice for him, much to my mother's chagrin, as it left her alone for long afternoons.

My parents had rented a house in East Hampton for the summer. This was the predecessor to the home we would buy out in Amagansett. My father would paint the door purple and plant pine saplings on the front hillside, beside an expansive and empty driveway.

The home we rented that summer stood a few blocks from a large and abandoned-looking house. Its shutters were closed. The paint was peeling. Dark and ominous, it loomed in a front yard that had been overtaken by weeds. My mother and I dubbed this the "rat house."

The "rat house" would come to symbolize my greatest fears that summer. Fear of the beetles in the basement of our rented house. Fear of being left alone with a stranger when my parents went out for the evening. Fear of the dark.

Yet during the day, the sun shone. There were trips to the beach, where I dug in the sand with a bright plastic pail and ate ice cream bars. And there was meditation.

My teacher was childlike. Had he been younger in years, we might have played together by the ocean. He was enthusiastic as he explained meditation.

I listened closely. Finally, I was discovering the grown-up technique that my parents practiced behind closed doors.

I felt as if I were receiving the wisdom of the ages.

Perhaps, I thought, meditation would be the answer to my shyness, to my feeling always a bit out of place.

As was the fashion with the New York City set, I had been raised by a nanny. I wasn't an unwanted child. This was just what people did on the Upper East Side of Manhattan.

I adored Agnes. I learned to speak with a heavy French accent, like hers. I preferred imported cherry jam on my toast, as did she. And, I only wanted her to push my stroller.

I was like a doll, Agnes said. She treated me as if I had been her own child.

With Agnes

When I was three years old, Agnes suddenly left.

My parents told me that she had returned to Switzerland. There was also some complaint about the vast quantities of imported jam that she had consumed.

After Agnes' departure, I was left in the care of one new nanny after another. There was Ellen, and there was Helen, and then there was the eponymous Nanny.

When Ellen arrived on the scene, I refused to accept her. She was freckled, and wispy, and rather young. She had no idea what to do with a child who did nothing but cry in her presence.

Mom and Dad

As the months passed, however, I realized that I was not going to get rid of her. Nor would my tears bring Agnes back. I began to calm down. Perhaps, in a small way, I began not only to accept Ellen but also to like her.

And then, she was gone.

Others came and went. Nannys. Sitters.

By the time I was old enough for my parents to care for me, I had developed deep feelings of insecurity. It was hard for me to connect to people, to trust that they would stay. I did not go out of my way to develop friendships. Nor did my mother encourage me to play with other children. Instead, I spent a great deal of time alone in my room.

Certainly, this was an ideal scenario for a young meditator. Child monks may be left alone for much of the day with only one or two toys to play with. They meditate, and they grow up to be masters.

There, in a shaded room of our summer rental, my teacher explained the benefits of meditation. Letting go of thoughts could alleviate problems. Repeating the *mantra* would chip away at stress.

The technique seemed to be working for him. He appeared to be joyful and confident.

Soon, my teacher's voice quieted. He was about to impart the sacred syllable that would be my *mantra*. Before revealing the mystic sound, he instructed me not to share it with anyone.

"Can't I tell my father?" I asked. Although he was often behind the closed door of his study, my father was the one in whom I confided. My father burned bayberry candles and incense cones, stashed chocolate in his top desk drawer, and imparted to me the secrets of leprechauns and levitation. He understood things that my mother did not. Surely, the initiation would mean far less if I could not share the *mantra* with him.

My teacher shook his head. "You can't tell your father your *mantra*." He explained, "If you tell people your *mantra*, it loses its power."

And so, I became a member of the sacred society into which both of my parents had been inducted. Perhaps it brought us closer together. Still, we meditated apart from each other. Each in his or her own room. Alone with the mind and the *mantra.*

THE WORD MANTRA carries with it an aura of mystery. It evokes images of wooden beads, exotic incense, and robes. It brings to mind resonant chanting and sacred space, be it cave or temple or mountain hut, or perhaps some magical land known only through legend. True to my teacher's words, a personal *mantra* is a well-kept secret, with the stipulation that it will lose its power if shared with others.

Many take this power on faith. As an abstract sound, a *mantra* may make little sense to the mind. In fact, it's not supposed to. If it did, the mind would hold onto it with associations and imagery.

Mantra may also be a holy name, one that resonates with divinity and awakens the presence within us. Still, we need neither understand the sound nor believe in it to be free.

An old Indian tale tells of a thief whose life was transformed by the power of a *mantra* in which he didn't believe. Though born a *brahmin*, he fell in with a band of marauders. For years, he lived a life of remorseless debauchery, robbing men, women, and children alike.

One day, he dared to steal alms from a wandering saint. The saint felt compassion for the misguided man. He asked whether the thief thought that his family would be as happy to share in the consequences of his actions as they were in the goods that he brought back for them.

The man was shocked to find that his loved ones turned away at the question.

The saint then offered to initiate the thief with a *mantra.*

At this, the thief scoffed. "I cannot repeat a sacred sound," he said, "because I don't believe in the sacred."

"It's alright," the saint responded. "Do you see that Mara tree?"

The thief gazed at the tree with its dark foliage and graceful trunk. It was late in the afternoon, and the setting sun glinted through its branches, casting long shadows against the earth. The thief could see that the tree existed. It was no more mysterious or sacred than he himself was. And it was beautiful.

"Simply repeat the name of that tree," said the saint. "Mara."

This, the thief took to. As he continued on his way, he began to repeat *Mara, Mara* over and over again.

It's said that, in time, he sat so still and chanted the *mantra* for so long that an anthill grew up over him. Still, he remained unperturbed. Because he chanted steadfastly, the syllables manifested great power.

When he emerged from the anthill, the thief was glowing. He had realized that, though stealing might bring him wealth without work, other people's possessions would never satisfy him. In fact, no possessions could satisfy him. He devoted the rest of his life in service to all beings.

As he sank deeper and deeper into the space of the heart, he began to compose great hymns of joy and praise. In fact, he composed the *Ramayana*, the epic poem that tells the story of Lord Rama, his wife Sita, and their ever-faithful servant, Hanuman.

This thief-turned-sage was the poet-saint Valmiki. As he had repeated *Mara, Mara*, so Valmiki had begun to chant the name *Rama Rama*. So he had become enlightened, and a source of truth for all.

IT SEEMS ALMOST TOO EASY that one need only repeat a sound to realize freedom from fear and angst. Freedom from loneliness. Freedom from rage, frustration, or self-doubt. Freedom to feel beautiful. Freedom to engage fully with life.

Still, in India, many believe that the power of a name like *Rama* makes all things possible.

The same can be said for any *mantra*.

The word *mantra* is formed from the Sanskrit roots *man* and *tra*. *Man* refers to mind or thinking. *Tra* is a verb root meaning to protect, to save, to rescue, or to defend. It also means to support.

The word *mantra* has various interpretations. It is often understood to mean "that which protects mind." *Mantra* protects the mind from negative thinking.

Maharishi Mahesh Yogi: Founder of the Transcendental Meditation Movement, through which Swamini was initiated as a child. Photo by Alan Waite.

Another way of understanding the word *mantra* is "that which crosses over mind." In the West, we recognize the syllable *tra* as relating to the later Latin root *trans*, meaning "to cross over." The root *trans* appears in English words like transport, transfer, or even transcend.

Experientially, *mantra* allows us to reach a place of inner peace that is deeper than the mind. The sound can be thought of as a bridge by which we cross the endless desires of the ego to selfless inner fulfillment. We cross step by step. Breath by breath. Syllable by syllable.

Mantra may also be compared to a lifeboat in which we cross the turbulent river of emotion. We have faith, even as the waves dash against the side of the boat, that we will dock safely in the inner sanctum of peace.

However we understand the etymology of the word, chanting *mantra* leads to an experience that is beyond words.

Mantra allows the mind to relax, so that we can experience who we are beyond its wanderings into realms of memory, fantasy, emotion, and projection. We reach the resting place from which mind is born.

Mantra is simply a manifestation of this refuge as sound. Through *mantra*, we come into union with the source of all experience.

CHAPTER 2

The Ancient Myths of Mind

THE UNQUIET MIND LOVES TO WANDER into the past. Sometimes, it seems that we are particularly drawn to unresolved or painful memories. They're hard to stay away from. We still want to work the situation out, somehow.

When the past becomes our focus, however, we have difficulty dealing with what's happening in the present. This is ironic, because what's happening right now is quickly becoming the past. If we want to be at peace with the past, we need to live mindfully in the present. Still, mind is drawn magnetically to what is emotionally unresolved.

The focus of our mind can be compared to a magnifying lense. When a ray of sunlight is focused and magnified through a lense, its energy becomes so powerful that it might set a piece of paper ablaze, or perhaps even some kindling. Similarly, when we focus our attention on a distressing experience, we set our minds ablaze with emotion.

It's interesting to pause and notice that this past happening need have no hold over our experience now. It no longer exists. It has no shape, no sound, no taste, and no smell. It has neither size nor color. We cannot touch it.

The memory is less real even than a mirage that appears in the desert. Like a mirage, a memory shows itself to be no more than open space upon investigation.

Still, we revisit past incidents again and again, as if we were making a repeated pilgrimage. It's surprising that we become devoted to memories that are both ephemeral and painful. It is counterintuitive. Why don't we become absorbed in the blessings present in our lives instead?

Sufi saint Hafiz brings light to the subject in his poem "Stop Being So Religious."

> What
> Do sad people have in
> Common?
>
> It seems
> They have all built a shrine
> To the past
> And often go there
> And do a strange wail and
> Worship.
>
> What is the beginning of
> Happiness?
>
> It is to stop being
> So religious
>
> Like
> That.

Certainly, it can be helpful to learn from the outcome of our past experience. Where was the turning point in the situation? What could we have done differently?

Still, there is a tipping point beyond which thoughtful contemplation becomes rumination.

Scientists have discovered that the brain is stimulated by memory or imagination in the same way that it is by what is experienced in the present. Whether we are riding a roller coaster or thinking of riding the roller coaster, the brain is activated in the same way. We have an emotional experience.

Think back. Remember the anticipation of waiting on line. The slow and creaking climb of the little cart up the steep incline. The sudden dropping away of anything solid. Maybe it was exciting. Maybe it was terrifying. Often, we feel more than one emotion at a time. This is what makes our experience interesting.

Notice that as emotion arises, breath and body respond to the imagined scenario, as well.

Similarly, when we replay any memory, mind and body react as if it were happening in the present. If we think back to the event again and again, our system responds as though that event had occurred not once but many times. A sudden disappointment. The wild elation. We create an emotional rut with our ruminations.

We then react to the present according to our feelings about the past. Though we are standing on solid ground, we still behave as if the ground might drop out from under us at any moment.

COMPARING OURSELVES TO AN ELEPHANT may help us in understanding how to free ourselves from these outdated memories. This may seem ironic: It is said that elephants never forget.

In this case, that's exactly the point.

In India, a young and wild elephant is tied to a tree with a strong rope while in training. Try as he might, the elephant child does not have the strength to break free. As the elephant matures, he may grow large and strong. Now, however, he can be tied to the tree with a simple cord.

Although he has the strength to break the cord, or even to uproot the tree, the elephant has been conditioned from childhood to think that he cannot. Therefore, he does not try to free himself.

Because he does not try, he lives under the illusion that he is as he has always been. He does not discover that he has matured. He fails to realize his true strength.

It's sad and unnecessary, you might say. Still, many of us don't notice the tree of past conditioning to which we ourselves are tied. We live with certain expectations. More often than not, the beliefs that we carry on from a painful childhood keep us from living fully.

As adults, we may take our self-imposed limits for granted. What we can or can't do. Whether or not we are worthy of love. We believe in the ancient stories that have shaped our idea of who we are today as if they were dogma.

Awareness of this kind of thinking is the first step to freedom. When we realize that we are tied with the cord of an old story, we can begin to test its validity.

As we muster up the courage to explore the world, we discover our untapped potential. We realize with joy and amazement that we need no longer be bound by an outdated system of false beliefs. We can be free.

PAST EXPERIENCE may also be liberating. Returning to the unconditioned state of childhood innocence allows us to break the bounds of conventional expectation as adults.

When I was small, I used to watch cartoons in my father's study. I was particularly engaged by the Road Runner and Woody Woodpecker. They were high-energy characters who made joyful sounds.

As I enjoyed the animated episodes, so I took in the intermittent advertising.

It was the mid-Seventies. Popular commercials included those for Irish Spring soap and Baby Alive. At the time, there was also a commercial for the Three Musketeers candy bar that aired again and again. In it, Athos, Porthos, and Aramis stood together in a hot-air balloon. One for all, and all for one. As they bit into their candy bars, with the nougat so light and fluffy, the balloon rose into the air.

Because eating the candy bar preceded lift-off, I mistook the sweet for the cause of flight. I became a big fan of Three Musketeers bar. Each time I took a bite, I waited to float up into the air.

When this didn't happen, I enhanced the possibility of flight by jumping off of things. I jumped from the seat of my small yellow chair. I jumped from low rungs of the jungle gym in the playground.

All to no avail.

Still, I was convinced that I could fly.

Perhaps this belief was compounded by a love for Peter Pan, genies who rode flying carpets, and our family *guru*, whose teachings on levitation my father practiced regularly.

With Mom in Dad's Study

My father was my childhood hero. Although he had a sudden temper, he could also be a magical person. Together, we journeyed through boardgame lands of candy and built log cabins with elaborate anterooms and three chimneys. We hunted for the elf who had snuck off with the missing puzzle piece. We made trips to Central Park, where we planted seed pods and watched, over the weeks, for a tree to grow.

In the afternoons, however, my father was behind closed doors. He was meditating. As my father progressed in his practice, a large beige mattress appeared on the floor of his study. He never slept on this mattress. Instead, he sat upon it to practice *yogic* flying. And so, from a young age, I believed that I, too, could fly.

To *yogis*, levitation is not unusual. When the mind is clear, the body is light.

As we come to recognize the myths of limitation that mind creates, we free ourselves from them. We lighten up, so to speak. We return to a state of innocence. Our experience becomes as expansive as the sky. Then, anything is possible.

CHAPTER 3

The Crystal Ball

MY PARENTS used to dine out on Saturday nights at a festive Indian restaurant in mid-town Manhattan. The place glittered with twinkling lights and brass plates. One evening, a palm reader was wandering amongst the tables that were laden with spiced vegetables, yogurt, and chutneys. Although the sights and sounds of the moment were exotic, my mother was yet enticed by her future. She extended her palm for a reading.

The fortuneteller rocked back and forth, passing her hand over my mother's. She offered small insights into my mother's character and solemnly foretold that she would bear three children.

As a young wife, my mother was simultaneously overwhelmed and excited by the news. At the time, she was pursuing a graduate degree in Classics at Columbia University. A year or so later, I became her firstborn.

When I was five years old, I begged my mother to have another baby. My best friend had a younger brother. He was our mascot. I wanted one too.

After months of our campaigning, my mother complied. So was born my brother. To this day, however, my brother and I have no third sibling.

My mother is now sixty-five years old. Although she remembers the predictions of the fortuneteller, she laughs about them as dramatic imaginings that enriched the evening. The predictions had been entertaining but inaccurate.

Great meditators may expand in consciousness beyond space and time. Infinity is realized in the eternal moment.

So, they are able to see into both the past and the future.

Most of us, however, can't know for certain what will happen in our lives. We set goals and plan, almost as if we were sketching. Knowing that the lines may be erased and redrawn as further detail is filled in. We don't really know where we will be years from now. We can't even be sure of what the next minute will bring.

A Brother Is Born

Still, we look into the future as if we had some great insight or vision. As if we were fantastical fortunetellers. We are constantly polishing our crystal balls. We make predictions. Then, we live as if these predictions had already come to pass.

Often, we project fear and failure. Replace the variables for yourself in the following sentence: *I'd like to do X, but I'm afraid that Y will happen.* On a daily basis, we let doubts about whether or not we will succeed, or how we will be perceived, define the way we live. *I'd like to try painting, but I don't think I'll be any good at it. I'd like to get back in touch with an old friend, but she probably has no interest in seeing me.* So go the stories we tell ourselves. *I can't trust this person, because I'm sure I'll be disillusioned. I am afraid to love, because I don't want to give up my independence.*

The story of the mind knows no end.

The Greek philosopher Aristotle spoke of *telos*, or the job for which something is particularly designed. The word *telos* may be understood as an end, aim, or purpose. An object's *telos* is described in relation to how it will benefit us in life, or ultimately, how it will benefit the soul. For example, a chair is made to be sat upon, and the ear's function is to hear. So it seems that the simple purpose of the mind may be to make sense of the world as we experience it. To tell the story of our life.

My grandmother used to weave incredible tales of dragons and princesses and old gnomes on long journeys.

"Tell me a story," I would say whenever she tucked me into bed.

"Do you want a long story, or a short story?" she would ask. The question was a joke between us. I always wanted a long story. One thing my grandmother never asked, however, was whether I'd prefer a happy ending or a tragic one. It was a given that no matter how dire the imagined situation became, everything would be alright in the end.

With Mom and Grandma

We enjoy fairy tales that end happily ever after. We look forward to victory. The hero slays a terrifying monster and the kingdom is his. The princess discovers hidden treasure and all of her dreams come true. Lover and beloved find each other again and live forever in love. All who hear such tales are inspired.

Still, the stories we tell ourselves about the future often do not end well. The mind weaves a tale of distress or failure. We picture ourselves slain by the dragon, imprisoned by an old witch, or somehow abandoned.

It's important to recognize that the tale we tell ourselves about the future arises from imagination. Our story may be enchanting and full of *pathos*. It may draw others close to us, for we project the need to be saved.

Still, we can cut right through it. We need not be bound by the tale of distress that we have conjured up.

Remember, the *telos*, or purpose, of mind is to benefit the soul. Mind might as well be put to the use of bringing the experience of joy and freedom. This is the *teleion*, or ultimate end, of all intermediate purpose. Happiness.

As easy as it is to picture doom, we might purposefully imagine a brighter future. We can live as though things were going to work out just fine. In this way, we face temporary obstacles with confidence. We open to them as interesting learning experiences. We hone our skills. We grow with each challenge.

Ultimately, we let go of storytelling altogether. Then, victory is ours.

When we are released from our personal story, we experience the poignant beauty of life, just as it is. The freedom of being absorbed into the wondrous whole that is without beginning or end.

CHAPTER 4

Attachment and Loss

UNTIL WE LOSE OURSELVES in the bliss of the whole, we may experience feelings of unrest. Sometimes, it seems that we are doing battle with life. Really, it is the mind fighting against circumstance.

One of my favorite books is the *Bhagavad Gita.* In fact, I sleep with my head on the *Gita.* My teacher once said that if you do this, you will realize the wisdom of the book within your heart.

In the *Bhagavad Gita,* Sri Krishna reveals to the despondent warrior Arjuna how to find freedom from the story of internal strife. He is Arjuna's friend and charioteer.

Young Arjuna is at a crossroads. He is supposed to be doing battle to win his father's share of the kingdom. The catch is, he must go to war with his own family, with his cousins who would have the the wealth and power for themselves. Arjuna sees this as an impossible situation. Even if he is victorious on one level, taking the kingdom, so he will have lost his loved ones. Confused, he sits immoveable in the chariot on the battlefield called Kuruksetra, the Field of Action. It's a metaphor for the field of life.

What is the right thing to do? And if more than one way is virtuous or *dharmic,* then what is the best thing to do?

Sri Krisna tells Arjuna simply to do his duty. He then offers seventeen chapters worth of enlightened discourse as to how we can overcome our internal struggles to live a life of peace and fulfillment.

When speaking of emotional conflict, Sri Krisna names attachment as the main cause of our troubles: If we convince ourselves that we need to have something in order to be happy, not having that will upset us. Whatever it us. Not having that particular person love us. Not getting the job promotion. Not having the money to make our dreams come true.

Often, we become attached not only to acquiring things like love, recognition, or wealth, but also to keeping things as they are. We'd like to push the pause button, to freeze-frame our life, right here: Resting completely at peace in your embrace. Standing in front of a huge crowd and receiving an award. Relaxing on the porch with a thick blanket, a mug of tea, and the rain splashing onto the earth.

We resist change when we like things the way they are. We probably wouldn't trade any of these moments for being abandoned by a loved one or for sprawling drunk and vomiting on the bathroom floor.

Perhaps, however, we can hold all experience with an open heart.

This desire that we share, to keep things the way we like them, is something that we can gently laugh about.

The world around us is constantly transforming, and so are we. Like a river flowing between its banks, our lives are not the same from one moment to the next.

This is the beauty of the experience. Life cannot be grasped or controlled or made to stay. Life is irrepressible and untameable, and truly, we wouldn't have it any other way.

Still, we experience certain kinds of change as deprivation. *I had this thing that I loved, and now I don't have it anymore.* The classic experience of loss.

A fellow student in a poetry workshop once wrote the line, "Sometimes we lose our keys. Sometimes we lose our fathers."

Years later, her words still run through my mind. Feelings of loss, whether over something mundane or monumental, come from not having what we think we need.

A common response to loss, Sri Krisna tells Arjuna, is anger. We stamp our feet and insist that we deserve better. We rail against our lives, or the person whom we hold responsible for our distress. Or we fall into despair, not knowing what to do next.

Sri Krisna explains anger to be such a strong emotion that it brings about a kind of delusion. We are temporarily incapable of rational thought. As a result, we begin to act in ways that we normally would not. It's as though we have forgotten who we are.

Think of the way you feel when you are angry. The mind becomes agitated. This agitated mind leads to tension in the body. You may have noticed that, with anger, your heart begins to pound and your fists to clench. The quality of the breath changes. Perhaps you hold yourself in a different way—the posture becomes contracted, rather than expansive and open.

We feel uncomfortable with these changes. Anger is not our natural state. We may later apologize to a loved one, explaining, "I just wasn't feeling myself."

Perhaps Sri Krisna uses anger as a blanket term for the range of emotion that we experience when our desire is thwarted. We may feel anything from disappointment to fear, bitterness to jealousy, fury to numbness.

Sri Krisna tell us not to worry when these emotions come up. He goes on to say that by shining the gentle light of wisdom onto the emotions, we can realize our natural state of tranquility. When we experience and understand the emotion fully, then we become aware of a deeper truth. A truth of peace that is independent of circumstance.

LIFE IS a generous teacher. We are given ample opportunity to explore our reactions to not getting what we want, and to learn from our struggles with loss.

When I was fourteen years old, my grandfather died over the Thanksgiving holiday. My family canceled the gathering that we had planned. My mother and I flew to Florida for the funeral. The service was simple. My grandfather was cremated in a raw pine box.

When we returned home, my mother retreated to her room. She came downstairs only for dinner. She did not want to talk with my father, my brother, or me. Instead, she worked at her clacking manual typewriter to document her father's death.

Grandpa

I missed my grandfather. Now, it seemed that I had lost my mother as well. When we would see her in passing, she was withdrawn and somber. The loss of her father had distorted her experience. She was so focused on his absence that she could no longer interact with the rest of the family, who were both living and waiting for her to return.

It took months for her to experience the natural feelings of anger and depression that accompany grief, and finally, to accept the loss of her father. Months for her to return to her usual buoyant self. For her to return to the family.

My family's silence around the death of my grandfather made it difficult for me to process the feelings of grief, as well. We did not speak much of him. Each of us handled the loss in relative isolation.

For me, my grandfather's death was the beginning of a troubled adolescence. One of rebellion and turbulence. One of searching for a deeper meaning or purpose to life.

Perhaps it was with his death that my spiritual quest truly began.

HOWEVER WE EXPRESS our pain, realizing that it is there and looking for something to make things better is stepping wholeheartedly onto the spiritual path. There is no need to judge ourselves or to blame others for the mistakes we make in our search for meaning. We simply make ammends, resolve to live kindly, and keep walking, one step at a time, into the light of joyful awareness.

I learned later in life that loss can be a direct springboard to awakening.

A classic Buddhist tale tells of a young girl, Kisa Gotami, who was transformed through her experience of loss.

Beautiful and kind-hearted, she had the good fortune to marry a nobleman's son. Soon thereafter, she bore a child.

Death does not discriminate between the young and old, between the rich and poor. The child died in the midst of a stormy night.

Unable to accept her son's death, the young wife wrapped his body in a blanket and began to wander in search of a medicine that would cure him. She visited the marketplace and the apothecary to no avail. Losing her mind to grief, she sought out her neighbors, insisting that someone must have an herb to awaken her sleeping infant. Of course, no one had the power to bring her boy back to life.

Wealthy as the girl's husband was, he could not console her.

Finally, a kind friend suggested that the young wife visit Sakyamuni Buddha. So, the girl set off to the forest to find him.

In the presence of the Buddha, the girl felt the warm and golden glow of compassion. She bowed down before him and offered her plea. As she had done with her friends and neighbors, she begged for medicine to revive her child.

The Buddha beamed with his usual benevolence. He explained to the young mother that she would need to obtain the medicine herself.

The girl looked up in hope. No one else had known of such a medicine. Finally, here was a being who believed that the cure existed.

The Buddha advised Kisa Gotami to go out into the surrounding countryside and bring back a handful of mustard seed. In his compassion, he added, "Be sure to bring back the mustard seed from a home where no one has been lost to death."

This seemed easy enough, and the young girl agreed to do so.

She ate a square meal, slept deeply, and then set off to find the mustard seed. She knocked at door after door.

Mustard seed was easy enough to find. Yet, at each home that she visited, the family told her that in their house, too, loss had been experienced. A loved one had died.

Finally, the woman sat down alone. She relaxed into the gentle rhythm of her breath. Although her hands were empty, her heart was contented.

She realized that her experience of loss was shared by all. Those who are powerful. Those who are brilliant. Those who are awakened. Those who are ordinary. Any and all of us.

She faced the fact that each of us will one day die. She surrendered, and opened to the impermanence of the world.

Kisa Gotami blossomed in the light of her intensely painful loss. It inspired her to live according to a new set of truths, the Four Noble Truths as put forth by the Buddha.

> When we identify with the impermanence of the world
> and of our mind, we suffer.
> This suffering comes from grasping at a sense of self,
> from the insistent desire for what we mistakenly believe
> will make us happy.
> There can be complete and lasting relief from suffering.
> To awaken from suffering, we simply follow the path of *dharma.*

This path to liberation is known as the *aryastangamarga*, or the Noble Eight-Limbed Path. It includes the following:

> *Right View*: Worldly gain or pleasure is impermanent and cannot bring lasting happiness.
>
> *Right Intention*: In whatever we do, we are motivated to delight all beings with the truth of liberation.
>
> *Right Speech, Action, and Livelihood*: We cause no harm and do what we can to spread joy with all that we say, all that we do, and with the work in which we are engaged.

Right Effort: We allow no room in the mind for discouragement.
We pursue the path with confidence and enthusiasm.
Right Mindfulness: We pay careful attention to our thoughts,
words, and deeds, so that they are consistently virtuous.
Right Concentration: We focus on the clear light, or the inner beauty,
that is the true nature of all beings.

So, Kisa Gotami realized that, even in this world of transformation, we can live in the expansive space of freedom. Freedom from desire. Freedom from anger. Freedom from ignorance.

Freedom to live without hesitation.

As can any of us, she renounced all worldly attachment, and lived in service to the awakening of all beings.

CHAPTER 5

Be with What Is

TWO FRIENDS SHARE a pot of tea at a low table. They are enjoying the stillness of being together. The sun is slanting through a large window. On the table stands a delicate vase.

One of the friends speaks. She notes the beauty of the vase, with its finely painted blossoms.

"Look closely," says the other friend. "This vase is not decorated with flowers, but rather, with the jaws of a fierce lion."

Neither friend is right or wrong. Each expresses what she sees from her particular perspective. A vase may look completely different from the opposite side of a table. Beneath the painted designs, a vase is plain clay. Within, the vase is empty space.

Similarly, we experience a situation according to our point of view. Our shifting emotional impressions. A mental experience that is not definitive or lasting. Meanwhile, the circumstance itself does not have inherent or definitive meaning. It is not bad or good. It is understood differently by different people at different times.

Beneath the ornamentations of personal experience and the object or circumstance is the basic teaching that we need to receive.

Ultimately, we experience *sunyata*. Emptiness. Not a void, but the experience of being free of mental and material phenomena.

When we realize the openness of experience, we are able to be with what is. Really, what else is there to do?

WHEN I WAS SIXTEEN years old, my father became dissatisfied with life. The change seemed to come without warning.

I had spent that summer on a foreign exchange program in France. I lived with a family in a rural village in Normandy. After six weeks of feasting on ripe cheeses and various kinds of crepes, crossing the border to dance in Belgian *boites de nuit*, and tuning my ear to the musical French language, I landed back in the LAX airport.

I had enjoyed the trip but missed my family. I had spoken with my mother only a few times during the summer, though she had written to me frequently. My father had never been at home when I called.

My parents were now standing at the airport gate together. I walked towards them with a duffel bag slung over one shoulder. It was stuffed with the leather jacket I had bought in Dijon, as well as tins of *bonbons a la violette*. These could not, I assumed, be found in Los Angeles.

My mother's expression was hidden by her oversized sunglasses. My father was shifting uncomfortably. My brother stood a short distance away.

I watched as the other students from our group were being hugged and kissed by their families.

Clearly, something was wrong here. For a moment, no one said anything.

Then, my mother spoke. "Dad moved out."

Learning to Drive on the Santa Monica Pier

The four of us returned to what we had known as home. We ate an awkward last dinner together, before Dad left for his beachfront hotel.

Soon after, he remarried. This was painful for my brother and me. We now saw him only on rare occasions. He and his wife seemed to feel ambivalent towards us. On our visits to their new home, we felt like guests.

From my brother's and my perspective, this change brought about much suffering. We missed the family time spent hiking in the mountains, making board game pilgrimages to Jerusalem, and reading aloud the lively anecdotes of British veterinarian James Herriot. Dad had always been the instigator of family adventure. As he moved on with his life, however, he adopted new interests. He became like someone we no longer knew.

Initially, my brother and I expressed our pain and rage through clever pranks. Programming a computer to dial his new telephone number every two minutes did nothing to repair the relationship. Nor did egging the garage door or having ten anchovy-topped pizzas delivered for his dinner.

In response to these efforts to get his attention, our father became enraged.

As I had when I was a child, I felt that I belonged nowhere. The ground was shifting beneath my feet. It was as though there had been a death in the family. I was left in the midst of a gaping and ragged void.

Still, my father had not died. He had chosen to leave. He had left not only my mother but also the family.

I was hurt, and I was furious. Love was supposed to last forever. This had been promised by every book and movie. It had been a lie. Life had betrayed me. God had betrayed me. All meaning seemed to be lost.

LOOKING AT A SITUATION from a bird's eye view, we often see that what brings sorrow to one may bring joy to another. When change brings us sorrow, one way to alleviate the suffering is to expand our perspective. We can look beyond personal loss to recognize the joy that has come into someone else's life. In this way, we share in these blessings. Sakyamuni Buddha taught this way of thinking as a means to heal the heart. He called it *mudita. Mudita* means empathetic joy. It means rejoicing in the virtues and blessings of others. It also means boundless joy.

Years later, I came to understand that my father had needed to live in a different way.

His new wife was not the reason for our estrangement.

She was, in fact, like a child herself. She needed caretaking. There was another side to her story.

My father's new wife had lived a life of great suffering. She had worked hard to recover from years of depression and addiction. My father, too, is a recovering alcoholic. Together, they enjoy each other's company, sobriety, and new altruistic interests.

By expanding my perspective to share in their virtues and happiness, I began to heal from the loss that had been tearing at my heart.

In so doing, I was able to begin again. To accept the situation. To explore a different kind of relationship with my father and also with his wife. Such is the beauty of *mudita.*

We sometimes think of feeling someone's pain. We have sympathy for someone who is struggling. Perhaps we understand the difficulties and want to help.

When we experience empathetic joy, however, we share in someone else's happiness. As we feel unselfishly happy for another, we too become joyful. We experience a generosity of heart. We let go of feeling that we have somehow lost out in the situation. We let go of corrosive emotions like jealousy and anger.

It is said that light and darkness cannot exist in the same place. When we light a single candle, the flame dispels the darkness around it. Similarly, when we light our minds with a single thought of joy, we are relieved of painful emotion.

As I released mind into the space of *mudita*, I began to accept the situation. Insisting on what was not had been creating intense suffering. This new arrangement did not match my idea of how things should be. It did not look like the family that I had grown up with. Still, it was not completely terrible.

People had benefited from this change. My father and his new wife were both happy. Their friends were happy. Even with this sudden and drastic change, I could be happy, too. Whatever this picture looked like, I was a part of it.

SO IMPORTANT is *mudita* to peace of mind that it is named as one of the Four Immeasurables, or the *brahma viharas*. These are the divine abodes of mind.

The *brahma viharas* offer refuge to the troubled mind. They include not only empathetic joy but also equanimity, lovingkindness, and compassion.

Each and any of these is an antidote to the emotions that bring the experience of distress. We can relax our suffering minds to rest in these infinitely expansive states.

Our disturbing emotions are like the smoke of a campfire. If we stand too close, the smoke is choking. It's hard to see or to breathe through it.

As we step back, allowing the smoke to dissipate into open space, the air around us clears. Then, we can breathe freely and enjoy the warmth of the fire.

These four boundless "feelings" are the immeasurable space into which we can release the emotions that choke us up.

Joy. Equanimity. Lovingkindness. Compassion. There are no limits to any of these.

Traditionally, lovingkindness is said to be the taproot of the other three. As we move through the spontaneous dance of life, however, the heart awakens in ways that are unpredictable. Experience is a true guide, balanced by deep respect for tradition.

For some of us, equanimity may be a stepping stone to lovingkindness. Equanimity, or *upekkha*, is about freeing ourselves from the personal story. We don't hold on to solid conclusions. When disappointment or hurt arises, we know that the world will not end because of what has happened "to us." Nor do we become elated when we experience good fortune. All worldly experience is passing.

We remain steady. We remain calm. We remain grounded.

We open to the bigger picture.

Taking refuge in equanimity, we discover the balance within by realizing the balance of the world around us. There is an interconnectedness to experience. The various events that play off of each other are intricately interwoven, so that each of us can realize what we need to, in order to be free.

We can trust in the process. Really, we have no choice but to do so. Life happens as it happens. Changing circumstance is often beyond our control.

As we begin to notice the ways in which events play off of each other in the world, we develop an internal sturdiness. A steady feeling of well-being.

I like to practice equanimity through the *yoga* postures. I work particularly with balancing poses during difficult times. When we're standing with one foot off the ground, or holding ourselves up on our hands, it's tempting to cling or to clench in some way. To tighten the jaw. To hold the breath. To have a very serious look on the face.

After all, trying to balance is nerve-wracking. There is the possibility of failure. Of falling. Of getting hurt.

We may feel these same tendencies when we struggle to find equanimity in our ever-changing lives. Off the mat, the same principles apply. To balance body and mind, we need to relax. We find a steady focus, and we breathe. We open to the possibility that the pose life puts us in can be easy, and suddenly, it is.

Equanimity goes hand in hand with lovingkindness, *metta*. There's some chicken-and-egg discussion over these two. Does a balanced perspective allow us to feel lovingkindness, or is it the other way around?

The answer to this question may depend on whether we are coping with a situation through analysis or through the heart. Sometimes, analysis of a situation can open the heart. When we are able to feel this glowing warmth of the kind and loving heart, then everything else seems naturally to fall into place.

Twenty-five hundred years ago, Sakyamuni Buddha sent a group of monks into the forest to meditate. Within a short time, the monks were accosted by mischievous spirits, or perhaps their own deepest fears, desires, and insecurities. The same distractions that we may face in our lives, today.

The monks returned from the forest to share these difficulties with their teacher.

The Buddha was unfazed. He sent his students back into the same forest. He did, however, offer them protection. He offered a teaching on *metta* as a way to deal with their fears.

Metta, or lovingkindness is to wish well for all beings. We don't pick and choose. This is how lovingkindness differs from personal love. Lovingkindness is more expansive than romantic love. It is more inclusive than love for our family or friends. Lovingkindness is unconditional.

Metta is akin to what *yogis* call *maitri. Maitri* is unqualified friendliness. *Maitri* is beyond preference for someone who has been especially kind to us or with whom we have good times. To rest the mind in *maitri* allows us to feel warmly towards those whom we have never met, or people with whom we have had painful dealings.

"How do I do this?" we might ask.

It's a good question, and the answer is simpler than we imagine it to be.

We begin with the feelings of friendliness or warmth that arise naturally, when we are with people who are close to us. People with whom we do have good times. People who love and want to support us, and for whom we feel this in return.

Then, we consciously bring these spontaneous feelings of lovingkindness into situations where that emotion might not immediately arise.

We exercise the mind and the heart. We nourish the feeling of radiant warmth by spending time with people we love. Our family and friends. Our teachers and students. People who make us laugh.

People who have really been there for us. Then, we recall the feeling of loving and being loved when somebody insults or ignores us.

Rather than letting mind run around in circles of fury, we seat it firmly upon the cushion of lovingkindness. We stop mind from elaborating on how we have been wronged and return it to the seat of *metta* over again, until it is comfortable with the situation.

In this way, we experience *metta* to greater and greater degrees. This helps the mind to stabilize. In turn, the mind with a balanced outlook on life is easily established in *metta*.

Through *metta*, we expand into the space of great compassion. *Karuna*. We are no longer concerned with what we can get but think of what we can give, for to give is to be fulfilled. We do whatever we can to delight those around us. We discover within the heart infinite altruism. We are awakening.

My teacher would often say, "Where there is love, there is no effort." Perhaps she meant that we ourselves become immeasurable as a source of goodness for all beings. We feel and express genuine benevolence for all beings, under any and all conditions. We shine like the sun. To live with this kind of radiance is to be an expression of truth in the world.

IF YOU ENJOY LANGUAGE and mental acrobatics, it's interesting to notice that these four liberating emotions, joy, equanimity, warm-heartedness, and compassion, are also named by *yogic* sage Patanjali as means to realize peace of mind.

In the *Yoga Sutras*, Patanjali matches these four liberating emotions up with particular situations: *Maitri karuna mudita upeksanam sukha dukha punya apunya visayanam bhavanatah citta prasadanam*.

Patanjali suggests that we be friendly with happy people, compassionate for those who are suffering, joyful for those of great merit, and neutral towards those who cause harm.

It's easy to understand why.

We like spending time with people who feel fulfilled. Happy people. Those who take joy in the play of life are good company.

These are beings who inspire us and who share our values. Maybe they even understand our vulnerabilities and help us to laugh at ourselves. Maybe they misplace their keys, or lose their cool once in a while, just like we do. We don't need our friends to be perfect, nor do we need to be perfect, in order to be happy. *Maitri.*

For those who are suffering, we feel compassion. We don't ignore or avoid their situation. We offer whatever we can in service to their awakening. Those who are suffering can be our greatest teachers, as is the suffering that we too experience. Only by embracing the balance of experience can all beings awaken. *Karuna.*

And then there is selfless joy. Joy arises not only from our own successes but also from everyone's blessings. When we are joyful for others, we free ourselves from the net of jealousy. We ride the powerful wave of good fortune that is carrying us all home to the heart. *Mudita.*

Lastly, if someone were to deliberately behave harmfully, we would then be unconcerned. We don't dwell on these kinds of situations. Perhaps, however, we pray for his or her happiness. Someone who causes harm is suffering in the darkness of ignorance. Wise and happy people don't hurt others. A small aside: If we are brave-hearted, we might consider our part in these painful situations. Taking responsibility is empowering. *Upeksana.*

Such are the four boundless emotions. Refuge for the troubled mind. Nurturing these qualities is a fool-proof system for dealing with any challenge that arises. This means that any of us can do it.

We can be liberated from our suffering. We can feel connected again. The heart that has been broken by life will begin to heal. So, we open beyond the pain of immediate personal loss to the greater expanse of gentle awareness.

To be with what is begins with accepting change and circumstance, but we don't stop there. To truly be with what is is to connect to a deeper truth. The truth of living as a part of the whole, awakened and in utter freedom.

CHAPTER 6

The Art of Relationship

AS WE EXPAND IN CONSCIOUSNESS, we begin to appreciate the people in our life as if we were artists. We become finely attuned to detail. We notice the delicate play of light and shadow. We look not only at a person or situation, but also at the space around it.

My father and I used to frequent the Museum of Modern Art. We would often visit a room of wall-too-wall Impressionist paintings. The Monets were his favorites, and so they became mine, too. Haystacks. Poplar trees. Painted again and again in different lights and during different seasons. The same thing seen in new ways. Purple in the sunset. Crisp in winter's snow and shadow.

As I grew older, my interest in painting expanded to include experimental film. Theorists of the 1960's such as Sigfried Kracauer suggested that the purpose of art is to "make strange" what is familiar. Kracauer explored in film the extreme close-up. What is it like to become so intimate with what is ordinary that it becomes unrecognizable, and so transcendent?

Artists break through traditional ways of looking. Artists lead us to see the same old thing as being suddenly fascinating. So, we are freed of conditioned response. We become truly present with the experience.

When we live our lives as if we were artists, we experience relationship in a way that is suddenly fresh. Particularly relationships about which we have had a fixed opinion. Those that we have rubber-stamped, filed away, and perhaps even discarded.

Artists like Marcel Duchamp saw beauty in "found" objects. Someone else's garbage. Duchamp's readymade sculpture "Bicycle

Wheel" is known throughout the world. Something that had been discarded is now appreciated as a thing of beauty.

So too, we need reject nothing and no one.

To live in harmony with those around us, we can come into the moment such that conditioned response no longer exists. No past. No future. Just the joyous present. This is the way that children play.

As we mature, we can also open up to the bigger picture of relationship. A view that extends beyond the limitations of our particular or most recent interactions with a person. We expand our perspective to see someone in different lights and seasons.

Knowing more about people allows us also to feel respect and compassion for them. We can understand their relationships with others besides ourself. We can appreciate their positive qualities. We learn to accept the whole being.

It is important to realize that the archetypal stepmother may also be a beloved wife and a dependable office manager. The dishonest shopkeeper may be a poor but devoted family man. Each of us is simply trying to be happy in the best way we know how.

A friend once brought out a photograph that she covered over with her hands. All that showed in the space I could see was darkness. Focusing on this small part of the picture, anyone would have thought that the photo was a bleak portrayal of something unrecognizable.

My friend slowly removed her hands. I saw then that the darkness had only been a part of the cloak worn by a kindly saint. Suddenly, the darkness made sense. The bigger picture revealed benevolence.

CHAPTER 7

Cool Sunglasses

WHEN I WAS A JUNIOR in college, sunglasses with lenses of all colors were the rage. These could easily be found at the drugstore on the outskirts of Ithaca, New York.

One of my friends liked to wear a pair of yellow-tinted shades, when we headed out in the evening. The strappy black dress she wore with them was actually a nightgown. It had cost a fraction of what a designer evening gown would have, but it looked like the real thing. We were twenty years old and playing dress-up.

I wore my sunglasses during the day, with a pair of faded blue jeans. Standing in front of the spinning plastic tower, I had tried one pair after another. Red lenses seemed too bright for daily use. Green sunglasses looked nice in hand, but when worn, the sky appeared to be indistinguishable from the grass. I did not want to be earthbound. I finally decided on blue-tinted lenses. The color was calming. It made the sky look deeper. If anything, it brought heaven down to earth.

Wearing these shades created a new reality, both externally and internally. The sunglasses were not only about how we would appear to others, but about how we would see the world.

I think sometimes of Hans Christian Andersen's tale of *The Snow Queen*, in which a child named Gerda sees the world through a metaphoric lense of great beauty. Her vision is not sentimental. Her heart is pure, and her mind, innocent. She gives people the benefit of the doubt. She focuses on love and gratitude in her relationships.

Gerda's view of the world contrasts with that seen in the mirror of an evil hobgoblin. His is a mirror of distortion, in which all that is pure and good appears to be ugly.

One day, the hobgoblin decides to carry the mirror up to heaven. He imagines that the angels might see themselves reflected in it and find themselves abhorrent. Higher and higher he rises. He is delighted.

As he rises, the mirror begins to shake and shiver with laughter. It too is gleeful. Suddenly, however, the looking-glass slips from the hobgoblin's hands.

The mirror falls back to the earth below. It shatters.

Shards of its distorting glass scatter in all directions. Bits of the mirror fall into people's eyes. The glass pierces people's hearts. So, they become hard and cold. They see themselves and the world around them distorted by the broken lense of selfishness.

When a bit of the hobgoblin's mirror blows into Gerda's playmate Kay's eye, he turns on his family. Wandering alone in the streets, he is abducted by the Snow Queen. The beautiful sorceress freezes Kay's heart until it is like a lump of ice.

Upon his disappearance, the town mourns Kay as dead. Gerda, however, is convinced that he still lives. In her faith, she embarks on a search to rescue him.

After a long journey, Gerda finds Kay sitting cold and alone in the Snow Queen's palace. At first, he fails to remember her. Gerda is heartbroken. Still, she persists. She can't blame him for being aloof. He is so cold that he can no longer feel anything.

At the sight of him, so alone in the ice palace, Gerda bursts into tears.

Her tears move Kay. He too begins to cry.

As tears flow from Kay's eyes, the shard of distorting glass is washed away. His innocent view of the world is restored. He remembers who he is and all that he loves.

OUR THOUGHTS bring on mood that can be compared to a pair of colorful sunglasses, or the reflection of a distorted mirror. Just as these lenses change our view of the world, so mood informs our experience of it. When we are enamored with someone or something, nothing gets us down. We feel invincible. In contrast, when the mind is disappointed or angry, all of life seems bleak. We take no joy in the simple pleasures that usually uplift us. And when the mind is frustrated, we experience the world as something against which we need to fight. A routine comment may set us on the warpath.

The *Dhammapada*, a collection of Sakyamuni Buddha's teachings for daily living, opens with this simple truth: "Our life is shaped by our mind."

Conventional understanding assumes that things happen the other way around. We believe that what happens in the world causes us to feel a certain way. The Buddha's teachings, however, turn experience around. They offer us a means to awaken by looking at the collective aspects of our experience. The causes and conditions that come together in a certain way at a certain time. The interplay of our internal experience with external circumstance. Namely, the role that mind plays in shaping our understanding of ourselves and the world around us.

As we look into the mind with honesty and tenderness, we realize the truth of the Buddha's words. Emotion doesn't arise from a particular situation. Our experience of mood comes from the mind's reaction to external circumstance, from the imprints of our past actions.

We know this to be true, because two people can go through a similar situation and respond in completely different ways. Whereas one person may become furious, another is humbled. One may become discouraged, while another is enlightened. We experience feelings of anger or forgiveness, dejection or love, jealousy or admiration, or any color of emotion, based upon the nature of our thoughts as the mind reacts to the world around us.

This is good news. We are not victims of circumstance. We can be free of suffering. We have full choice in how we respond internally to any given circumstance.

Taking an interest in the workings of mind like this is akin to removing the colorful sunglasses. We begin to see things for what they are. Not only in the external world, but also within.

We recognize change in the world around us, as well as the changing interpretation that mind brings to that experience. Then, we are able to experience something else. Truth.

Truth is that which does not change. In our search for truth, we move through all that we find to be untrue.

Neti neti. Not this. Not this.

We stop pretending, and we stop clinging to unverified beliefs.

Then, we experience that which illuminates the fluctuating experience of mind. We discover a radiance within that remains unaffected by both the events of the world around us and the mindstream. So, we become a source of freedom for anyone who happens to be in our presence.

CHAPTER 8

The Film Projector

OUR MENTAL EXPERIENCE of the world around us can be compared to a film that is being projected. The mind superimposes personal drama onto an event that is as neutral as a blank screen. The light shining through the projector is untroubled consciousness. Without this light of awareness, the mind could not project its imaginings onto external situations.

This light remains constant throughout our changing experience. Yet, so often, we identify with the emotional projection, rather than with the awareness of an experience. Again and again, we get caught up in the drama that mind creates. An internal drama that may have nothing to do with what's actually happening.

A friend needed to have a picture scanned for a postcard she was creating. She took the image to a neighborhood copy center. The store offered all kinds of services. They created logos. They printed business cards. As a result, they were quite busy. My friend left the piece of artwork to be scanned overnight.

The following morning, she returned to retrieve the image on disc. She was pleasantly surprised to find no line at the counter. She greeted the salesperson with a smile, and he set off to find her file.

Before he could find her file, however, a crowd began to gather at the counter. Someone called for help with pricing for a photo montage. The man obliged. He offered pricing details on glossy paper of different weights and foam board, and left the client to consider the options.

Again, he turned to find my friend's disc. At this point, someone else approached the counter with a question about work she was doing at a design station. She was being charged by the minute for use of the computer and its software, so the man left the counter to help her.

Clients continued to gather at the counter, jockeying for position.

My friend was irritated. *He's ignoring me, because I'm not assertive enough,* she said to herself. One thought led to another. *He doesn't take me seriously, because I'm being nice. I need to say something that will get his attention.* She remembered one of her neglectful mother's favorite sayings: *The squeaky wheel gets the grease.*

By the time the man returned to the counter, she had worked herself up. She was ready to let him know that she was not the kind of person to be ignored.

Before she could speak, however, the man smiled at her and said, "It's crazy here today. If one more person had made a demand of me, I wouldn't have been able to handle things. Thank you for being so patient." He then handed her the disc.

My friend was surprised. Her mind had fabricated the story that the man had been ignoring her, when really, he had been appreciating her. Luckily, he had spoken before she had.

This kind of misinterpretation is common. It is so common that *yogic* philosophy offers a continuum through which we can understand our view of the world.

Philosopher, grammarian, and medical doctor, the sage Patanjali explained the whirling workings of mind, as well as how to realize inner stillness. Patanjali was scientific. He codified our ways of understanding according to five categories: Valid cognition, misunderstanding, hallucination, sleep, and memory. *Pramana, viparyaya, vikalpa, nidra, smritaya*, he wrote in the *Yoga Sutras.*

When our experience of mind comes from *pramana*, or valid cognition, we understand things as they are. At least in a conventional sense. *Pramana* may come from clear and direct perception, logical inference, comparison, or the words of the wise. There is no problem here. More often than not, however, some level of misunderstanding distorts our experience.

In the cases of delusion, sleep, and memory, the difference between what the five senses might perceive and our mental cognition is quite obvious. Our ideas about what's happening don't match up with reality.

Simple misinterpretation, or *viparyaya*, on the other hand, is more challenging to discern. In a mind state of *viparyaya*, we are both lucid and conscious. We aren't delusional. We aren't dreaming. Neither are we in confusion about the past. Our misunderstanding is subtle.

It is, however, precisely because *viparyaya* is so close to clear perception that this kind of misunderstanding is tricky.

So powerful is *viparyaya* that it distorts our experience in much the same way that hallucination, dream, or memory might. Through *viparyaya*, we project our false beliefs out onto the world.

We then act according to our projections.

Remember, we might compare this way of living to screening a film. We experience circumstance according to our projections of mind. Our personal interpretation. Our misunderstanding. *Viparyaya.*

By understanding our misunderstanding, however, we can begin to live with greater compassion, for both ourselves and the people in our life.

WE REALIZE THE TRANSPARENCY of the drama when we begin to explore not only the projections of mind but also the different roles we play.

As we live in the movie of the mind, we identify ourselves in different ways, depending on whom we are with or what we are doing. Yet, relationship and action are always in flux. These are passing appearances. They are not lasting, and so they are not ultimately real.

A simple example of our relative role in life is family relationship. Many of us are both parent and child, or sibling and spouse. If we think of sitting at the holiday dinner table, we may be all of these things simultaneously, as well as aunt, cousin, and grand-niece. It's mind-blowing to think about this.

We turn to pass the mashed potatoes to our mother as a child, and then, as we lift the china gravy boat to pour for our brother, we suddenly assume a new role. This happens in a split second, in less time than it takes to enjoy a good mouthful of grandma's cooking.

Likewise, we may be both old and young, experienced and discovering, or even adored and disliked. These identities depend on circumstance and comparison. They are not innate.

With our role changing from moment to moment, the question then arises, *Who am I really?*

Truth is that which does not change. If we can play different roles simultaneously, then the deepest truth is that we identify with none of them.

Let's backtrack now, because it's important.

Again, the same can be said of our emotions. They are simply a projection of mind based on our interpretation of events. Remember, the world is like a neutral screen that is colored by our flickering ideas and feelings. If we become truly attentive, then we notice that emotion changes from moment to moment. From one breath to the next.

This is how we discover that both the roles we play and our emotional responses are created. They are a response to circumstance. They are not the deepest truth of who we are.

We are the clear awareness of our changing role and feelings. We are the one who is taking an interest in this movie of the mind.

A popular mind-bender is this. *If a tree falls in the forest and no one is there to hear it, does it make a sound?* To put things another way, if a movie is playing but no one is there to watch it, is there drama going on?

Paradoxically, in this case we discover that, because there is someone watching the movie, the drama is not really occurring.

We are the one who is watching the movie.

When we realize that we are the one who is watching the movie, rather than a character whose life is bound by the drama and the screen, then we can enjoy the experience.

Bhagavan Sri Ramana Maharshi: Bhagavan advised sincere seekers to follow the "I" back to its source. Through Self-inquiry, unalloyed happiness is realized. This is a direct path to liberation. Of chanting *mantra*, he again said to experience the Source from whence the *mantra* arises. Photo printed with permission from Arunachala Ashrama.

Watching a movie is enjoyable. We get comfortable. We settle into the plush theater seats with a tub of popcorn, a box of candy, and an ice-cold drink for a couple of hours of entertainment.

We like films, because we can have all kinds of adventures without taking the events too seriously. We may be intrigued by the romance gone awry, the impending battle, or the search for the grail. At the same time, we know that we are not really affected by the action that is playing out across the screen. We are relaxed and happy, sitting quietly in the darkened theater.

Similarly, it is possible to experience the cinema of life. When we don't get caught up in our role, we can engage with people in a way that is genuine. Without pretense. We need not be ensnared by their role either. We live in freedom, neither fearing rejection nor needing approval. Nor are we caught up in the drama, needing the storyline to go one way or another.

We awaken each morning, not knowing what the day will bring, yet ready for anything. Through it all, we are both fully engaged and liberated in the light of consciousness.

CHAPTER 9

Patience

WHAT ABOUT THOSE TIMES when we can't see through the projection of our mind?

Emotional response sometimes feels automatic. It's if life were playing a game of pinball, and we were the board. One reaction precipitates another. Lights and buzzers are going off everywhere.

We forget that we have a broad range of choices in how we can respond to a given circumstance.

Instead, we become self-righteous. We say, *This is what so-and-so did, to me.*

So uncaring. So unfair. That's how we feel about it.

We forget that the reactions are caused by the little metal ball that is getting banged around. Our ego. The sense of who I am, what I need, and, in fact, what I deserve.

The problem is, we can't see past the emotion of the immediate situation. We are lost in the fantabulous spectacle of how we have been wronged. If only we were truly present in the moment, without projecting or embellishing, experiencing the now would be just fine.

Because we're bedazzled by our personal story, however, we react in a way that is disproportionate to what's actually happening. We lose our temper, fall into despair, or give in to the wiles of desire.

Luckily, these reactions bring wisdom. When we have the courage to explore them with honesty and tenderness, we discover an inborn source of truth.

All we really need to do is to continue breathing.

Over time, we find ourselves able to relax the grip of immediate angst and need. We become willing to let life play out as it will.

We take refuge in patience.

AN OLD FOLK TALE tells of a farmer and his family who lived on a small plot of land with one horse in their stable. The farmer, his wife, and their son lived a simple life. They depended on the bounty of each season to fill their table.

One evening, a passing bandit snuck into the family's barn and stole their only horse.

"Alas," cried the farmer. "What will we do now?"

His wife was undisturbed by the sudden change in circumstance. "Wait and see," she said.

Within the week, their horse returned to the farm. He had broken away from the robber and had brought a band of wild horses back with him.

"Ah," cried the farmer. "Now, we are rich. We will never be hungry again."

The farmer's wife said simply, "Wait and see."

The next morning, the farmer's son set about trying to train one of the wild horses. He had little experience and so was thrown quickly. In falling from the horse, he broke his leg.

The farmer raised his arms to the heavens. "Without my son to help me work, how will I maintain the farm? Surely we will starve."

The farmer's wife just smiled and said, "Wait and see."

Days later, the village in which they lived went to war with a neighboring town. All young and able-bodied men were called into service. Because their son had a broken leg, however, he was spared from the dangers of battle.

"I see," said the farmer. "We are truly blessed."

The farmer's wife said only, "Wait and see."

The farmer's wife understood that we can't know immediately what a particular change will bring. Life is ever unfolding, like the petals of a delicate flower.

If we were to force open a bud, the flower would wilt without blooming. In the same way, we cannot rush through life's transformations.

We nurture ourselves and those around us with a steady and compassionate heart. This is the water and the sunlight.

We relax and allow the garden of life bloom in its own time.

DOES TAKING REFUGE IN PATIENCE mean that we don't try to improve things or have positive goals in life?

Definitely not. There is an easeful balance to discover, somewhere between receptivity and effort.

Returning to the battlefield of Kuruksetra in the *Bhagavad Gita*, we find Sri Krisna explaining to his disciple Arjuna that we must do our best in life, without insisting upon a particular outcome at a particular time. We try hard, and then watch the effects of our actions play out. We remain easeful and open in mind. Rather than creating solid conditions that are necessary for our happiness, we allow ourselves to flourish throughout all circumstance.

In the field of experience, we plant a seed through intentional action. We fertilize and water the seed with our thoughts and prayers, and perhaps with further action. We tend lovingly to the sprouting sapling.

Still, we may make these efforts only to harvest sour lemons instead of sweet peaches.

Or perhaps we harvest no fruit at all. The birds eat it, or our neighbor takes it in the dark of night.

The sapling to which we have tended may even wither and die, so that we need to begin again.

Even so, we need not lose patience. We need not sacrifice our natural state of peace to unexpected and passing happenings.

The sage knows to be prepared for any outcome. Therefore, the sage responds calmly and with kindness to any circumstance.

The wise one understands that the particular fruit of our labor is what each of us needs to experience, so that we can learn and mature. Bear in mind that what we think we need is not always what is best for us. All that we might wish for ourselves and the world is but a scant handful of the bountiful harvest that all will one day receive.

TRUE PATIENCE takes courage and strength. Even for one of divine nature.

A classic Hindu scripture, the *Srimad Bhagavatam* tells the story of a milk ocean that was churned into nectar. For decades, the world had been becoming a bitter place. People were no longer motivated to try new things, or even to succeed where they were skilled. They were failing to be kind to one another. As time went on, they began to cheat one another, in business and in relationship.

Even the animal kingdom was affected. Cows failed to give milk. Horses lost the spring in their trot. Birds sang half-heartedly. Meanwhile, harvests were sparse, and flowers bloomed with faint color.

The gods noticed that the world needed an elixir. To this end, they decided to churn the milk ocean of their heavenly abode into one of nectar. At the command of their hearts, they lifted the largest mountain that they could find. They carried it through the sky and dropped it into the middle of the milk ocean. They wrapped a strong and generous serpent about the mountain. Then, they divided themselves for the task. Some took hold of the serpent's head, while others held onto his tail. All began to churn.

The gods churned the milk ocean for days. As they did so, what came forth was not the nectar for which they had hoped, but multifarious demons. Horrific visions of fear, anger, despair, and pride. These were followed by greed and lust, jealousy and lies.

The gods were confused. All that they had wanted to do was to make the world a better place, yet things seemed only to be getting worse. They were meeting with continued resistance.

They did not, however, waver in the work that they had begun. They churned steadfastly.

The ocean frothed and boiled. Then, far more than demons came forth. Deadly poison began to spout from the sea. Those who had been hardest at work became afraid for their lives.

Nothing was going as planned.

Still, the gods continued. They followed the guidance of their hearts. They let go of their frustration and exhaustion. They allowed their minds to engage neither with the many demons, nor with death's poison. They continued simply because the churning needed to be done. The work became a meditation.

At last, the milk became lucid. The ocean glowed as if lit from within. The turbulent waves calmed, and the sea became one of foaming nectar. The world was revived.

The gods, too, were refreshed and satisfied.

The wise say that our true nature is divine. Awakened. So, we too can strive onward when we don't get the results that we had expected, immediately. Even as we are surprised to face further challenge to our truly benevolent intention.

Patience pairs with perseverance. Do you remember the old adage on perseverance? *If at first you don't succeed, try, try again.* The only certainty is that if we give up, we won't arrive in the here and now. If we keep trying, however, we may get a different interim result than we had been hoping for, but we will see positive change. Transformation.

Taking refuge in patience allows us to continue. The mind grows calm, as our effort is strong. Eventually, like the milk ocean, our mind becomes one of lucid nectar.

A WAIT-AND-SEE ATTITUDE gives us the chance to relax. Again, the initial outcome of our efforts is not important in the long run. Rather, life is about the way we handle the situations that are churned up by our best efforts. As we watch our personal demons spring forth to perform the dance of distraction, we have the opportunity to master our impulsive reactions.

Emotional maturity begins with awareness. We find the space to witness our reactions, rather than giving up or acting out. We let go of our initial response to a situation. We may let pass the second and the third reaction, as well. We have patience with ourself.

We watch our impulses arise as if we were appreciating an exotic tiger. We take in interest in the strength and grace. Still, we don't get too close. We don't know what might happen next. We observe the growling and prowling from a safe space. From the still point at the center. From the refuge of a loving heart. So, we tame the wild parts of ourself. We develop trust.

As we begin to trust our own strength in opening to emotion, we are able to take a true interest in the workings of mind. We notice with compassion the way one thought leads to another. We begin to understand the ways that thought motivates mood and behavior.

We pay attention to the feelings and allow destructive impulses to calm down without acting on them. Eventually, we gain confidence. We realize that, yes, we can remain steady. The uncomfortable feelings will pass, without our needing to do anything right now but relax.

Sufi saint Hafiz writes on this in his poem "The Vintage Man."

The
Difference
Between a good artist
And a great one

Is:

The novice
Will often lay down his tool
Or brush

Then pick up an invisible club
On the mind's table

And helplessly smash the easels and
Jade.

Whereas the vintage man
No longer hurts himself or anyone

And keeps on
Sculpting

Light.

As we acknowledge our strong reactions, allowing them the space and time to be absorbed into loving stillness, so we save ourselves from acting in ways that we will later regret. We save ourselves through patience from needing to piece together again the shards of our relationships and the fragments of our life.

Ultimately, life's churning yields realization of the ocean of nectar within our hearts. As the farmer's wife says simply, wait and see.

CHAPTER 10

A Gentle Turn of Mind

A COMPANION to the *Tao te Ching*, the *Chuang Tzu* tells of a man who tried to run away from himself. This man didn't want to leave behind everything about himself. Just certain parts of himself, like the clunking sound of his footsteps and his own dark shadow.

As he ran, however, the man noticed that the sound of his footsteps was becoming louder than ever, while his shadow had no trouble keeping up with him.

He decided that he must not be running fast enough. He picked up speed. Still, the faster he ran, the louder his footsteps became, and his shadow remained at his heels.

Finally, the man dropped from exhaustion.

In this moment of surrender, the sound of his footsteps stopped. Meanwhile, his shadow disappeared in the midday sun that shone directly overhead.

The man realized that running away had worn him out, but that sitting still and bringing his shadow into the light had liberated him.

We, too, may want to leave parts of ourself behind. We might feel the need to change ourselves and our lives in order to be loveable. In order to be happy.

We may want to run away from parts of our life that we don't know how to deal with, as if we were still a confused and angry teenager.

We run away, so to speak, in different ways. Sometimes, we run away by breaking off a relationship without explanation. At other times, we might turn to alcohol, drugs, shopping, food, sex, or anything else we use to mask the pain.

Then again, running away need not be dramatic or destructive. Sometimes, we run away by striving for worldly success. We try to compensate for our inner feelings of unworthiness by doing great things.

Still, with this kind of motivation, no matter what we achieve, there is more to be done. We could make more money or be better respected. We could be more intelligent, creative, or talented. Our projects could be more far-reaching.

So many things, we imagine, would make us happy.

Happiness is the holy grail. We all want to find relief from our suffering. From our feelings of being less than. From the haunting sense that we are not good enough and so cannot be loved.

When let go of the struggle and accept ourselves as we are, however, we discover the innate power to transform our experience. Sitting quietly, we realize with compassion the way our thinking patterns are affecting our lives. The heart opens in the warm light of awareness.

SAKYAMUNI BUDDHA taught that we can turn the mind to be free of the thoughts that cause us such suffering. He compared the spiritual seeker to an archer. Just as the archer aims an arrow, so one who wants to be free will aim the dissatisfied mind.

First, we let go of distraction. The call to do more, to get more, and to be more. We focus, so that the mind becomes sharp. One-pointed, like an arrow.

Then, we aim the mind towards what will bring peace.

The question is, to what do we turn the mind, initially, in order to be free?

You've most likely heard the adage about seeing the glass as half-full instead of half-empty. This kitchen wisdom has its roots in ancient teachings. Patanjali taught that when a disturbing thought arises, we can turn the mind to the opposite thought. *Vitarka badhane pratipaksa bhavanam.* So reads an aphorism from the *Yoga Sutras.* Bringing to mind a calming thought is similar to the way we might take mouthfuls of cooling *raita* to neutralize the effects of a *sambar* so heavily spiced that it makes our eyes water.

As we turn each upsetting thought around, soothing the mind with an alternate concept, so we change our way of relating to the world. We relieve our minds of negative thinking patterns, so that we can live a joyful and liberated life.

An art therapist I worked with on a detox unit found herself short on supplies one afternoon. This was only a momentary dilemma. Tina was a veteran in her field, inspiring social interaction and cognitive breakthroughs with what seemed to be simple and childlike projects. She had little tricks up her sleeve, like purposefully not putting out enough pairs of scissors, so that the patients would get into conversations through the need to share. I would sometimes stay on after the meditation group I had offered to learn from her.

This afternoon, Tina offered a project that was particularly innovative. On the large, round table, she placed a few pieces of paper and some magic markers.

First, we were to fold plain white paper into cubes. She then offered colorful construction paper squares on which to write positive sayings. These would be glued onto each face of the cube.

We sat all afternoon with nothing more than a few pieces of blank paper and some magic markers. We turned our minds from perceived difficulties to the truth of the heart.

Sitting around the table, we shared what we had written on our cubes. Some of the sayings that came up were these: *I am willing to try. Things can turn around. I am likeable. Love is real.*

I still have the paper cube I made that afternoon on my desk. A favorite reminder is that it's alright to make a mistake.

Tina explained that these cubes were like loaded dice. Whichever way they landed, you couldn't lose.

Of course, turning the mind in a positive direction is sometimes easier said than done. As with anything, from drawing to cooking to playing soccer, it takes practice to become skillful. The more we practice, the easier things get.

IN THE FACE OF CHALLENGE, we all have signature thoughts that arise. Some of us have a flair for the dramatic. Our first response to a difficult situation may span decades to come, as well as the workings of the universe. *I just can't handle it. I'll never get over this. How could God have let that happen?*

Others find a grim resoluteness. *It doesn't matter anyway. There's no point in trying to resolve this.*

To relieve the pain brought on by this kind of thinking, we begin by redirecting the mind in simple situations. Insecurities may crawl out from the dark corners of our mind when we are trying something new. Feelings of isolation might rear up when we feel momentarily unappreciated.

We learn by practicing with situations that aren't heavily loaded. A situation that doesn't have a long history behind it. An interaction with a person with whom we are less intimate.

A friend who worked in public relations fell into the ironic pattern of withdrawing from her personal relationships. She did so whenever someone spent a great deal of time with another friend. She noticed that, before she would pull back, mentally ending the friendship, she would experience deep feelings of rejection.

The thoughts of rejection would build upon themselves, as if her mind were laying brick and mortar, building a wall between herself and others. One thought piled upon another, hardening into an impenetrable belief system. Not only had a friend made plans to spend time with someone else for the afternoon, but he or she must also far prefer that person to her. Perhaps she was not loved at all.

This kind of thinking would lead her to withdraw. She would be so hurt as to turn down any future invitations, a sure means to push her friends even further away. The compounded rejection reinforced her belief that she had never been loved. Her prophecies were self-fulfilling.

She behaved like the lily in Rumi's poem "A Babbling Child."

A lily looks at a bank of roses
and wilts and says nothing.

Like the lily, this woman was overcome by feelings of inadequacy. She dwelt on feelings of separateness, the idea that she was somehow different than others and alone, rather than an awareness of her own beauty. A beauty that is the same in each of us.

When she realized the way her thinking patterns were affecting her relationships, however, she decided to free herself of them. She began to practice. She decided that she would turn her mind in the face of perceived rejection. She began by purposefully eliciting feelings of isolation in a situation that felt safe enough to explore her reactions.

One evening, she decided to try an experiment. She had been invited to a good friend's birthday party. The room was filled with people whom she knew and could easily approach. Still, she made a point of retreating to the hallway, just outside of the kitchen. From here, she could see and hear the festivities, though she was not a part of them.

As the old feelings of being unwanted arose, she was able to turn the thoughts around.

Certainly, the people at the party did want her company. After all, she had been invited. She had friends in the living room.

She also told herself that, though she was not included now, this situation was temporary. She could choose to change her circumstances at any moment.

She calmed herself down. Then, she consciously behaved in the opposite way to her usual manner. Rather than hanging back like a wallflower, she approached people warmly.

As she continued to practice in situations of greater and greater challenge, she repatterned her emotional reactions and her behavior. She turned her mind from its shrinking fears of being unwanted to the possibility that she was well-liked. She nurtured the idea that she was a necessary part of the social fabric.

She let go of the idea that if she were not the favorite, then she was nothing at all. She found a middle ground. She became able to tolerate being a part of a group without needing that validation of special attention.

She was then able to continue her relationships, even when she found out that she was not another person's closest friend. This left room for her relationships to grow. She needed less and had more to offer.

She succeeded in turning her mind from the sharp thorns of perceived rejection to the blossoming opportunities for expanding her social circle.

A circumstance that disturbs the mind like this is a gift. We might think of life as one big party at which we are being offered carefully chosen presents. If we receive each gift with gratitude, taking care to unwrap and fully appreciate it, we can benefit from it.

We may even feel gratitude towards the person or situation that has presented us with such a gift. After all, we have been given the opportunity to discover thinking and behavioral patterns that hold us back. In exploring these patterns with confidence and enthusiasm, we can transform our lives. We can awaken to live in boundless joy and freedom.

CHAPTER 11

Kind Action

TURNING THE MIND makes sense not only in the context of personal experience, but also in the bigger philosophical picture. Eastern spirituality emphasizes *karma*. *Karma* is the law of causality. *Karma* explains why we may be going through particular difficulties: We have something to learn from them.

There is a purpose to this passing suffering. We can grow stronger from the challenges. We can be free.

According to the natural forces of *karma*, our present experience is born of past action. What we have offered into the world returns.

The idea of *karmic* return is akin to a simple discovery made in physics. Sir Isaac Newton's third law of motion explains that every action has an equal and opposite reaction.

This idea is easy to observe in the physical world. We toss a tennis ball up into the air and it comes back to us. If we aren't paying attention, the ball may whack us in the head. If we're paying attention and see it coming, then we can catch it in our hand.

Awareness and focus are important. If we want to catch the ball, we need to realize what is happening and then meet the situation with confidence.

This principle applies not only to tossing a tennis ball up into the air and having it return to us, but also to any action that we might offer to the world. This includes what we say, or even what we think.

To be on the receiving end of our actions is truly a blessing.

What better way to learn from our mistakes than to become the recipient of them?

At first, we may be motivated to work on ourselves, so that we can be spared unnecessary pain. We try not to act harmfully, because we don't want this kind of action coming back to us. We want our relationships to be more loving. We want to be more successful at work. We want life to be easeful and enjoyable.

When we allow our emotional reactions to pass without acting them out, we are saying, *I want to connect out of love rather than anger, fear, desire, or any other delusion of mind.*

When we take enough interest in a painful situation to stay connected, we are really saying, *I too may hurt people. I may even have hurt you. Still, I have the best of intentions, so I understand that you too must have good intentions. That, like me, you just want to be happy.*

When we work hard to overcome our hurtful tendencies, we are saying, *I am willing to abide in awareness for the greater good. Such is my commitment to this relationship and to the world.*

We are saying, *May all beings be free of their emotional sufferings. May all beings be happy.*

CEASING TO CAUSE HARM is only the first step. Taking the idea of *karma* to the next level, we discover that we actually have the potential to create a joyful life for ourself, as well as for others. Then, we take the positive action of offering blessings in whatever way we are able to.

Yes, according to the principles of *karma*, if we are kind to others then kindness will return to us. So, we begin to plant the seeds of compassionate action.

Soon, however, we realize that we don't need to wait for a return on our "good deeds." The act of kindness becomes fulfilling in itself. The power to make positive change in the overall experience is its own reward, as is the simple beauty of connection.

One afternoon, I found myself in line at the grocery store with a full shopping basket. The people ahead of me also had full baskets. Fruit. Bread. Greens. Pasta. We were each on a mission to satisfy ourselves.

Perhaps you've noticed that the checkout person has a repetitive and continuous job to do. On this afternoon, she swiped item after item over the electric eye, as one person after another passed through, without taking notice of her.

Blip. Blip. She had been standing for hours. Her hands were tired. The store was cold. And yet, the experience could be suddenly transformed.

On this afternoon, I smiled and said, "How are you today?" She was surprised. And then she was joyful.

Connection is powerful. When we smile at somebody, he or she smiles back. We share a transformative moment. Impersonal routine shifts, on both sides.

The waiting on line and the mechanical swiping.

Our interaction has meaning. There is mutual appreciation. A moment of union.

We may both share that smile with the next person we see. The joy ripples outward, exponentially.

A call to kind action may be the common thread woven through all religious and spiritual traditions. Across time, in different languages, and with various images, the masters have all said the same thing. If we wish to live in a peaceful world, we begin with ourselves, by behaving kindly in the present moment.

So, the simplest action is a powerful prayer that affects not only our immediate experience but also the world around us. Our every action can be a prayer for liberation. Freedom for all. It begins with a gentle turn of mind.

CHAPTER 12

Mantra and Mood

THROUGH PERIODS of repeated loss or prolonged distress, turning the mind may not come easily. We may feel that we are being carried away by catastrophic thinking, as if we were a small raft in the raging rapids. The painful thoughts may build upon themselves, like a snowball that picks up size and speed as it careens down a mountain.

At this point, we can let go of focusing on each individual moment of upset. It would be unnecessarily difficult to find a plausible opposite to each disturbing thought that crosses the mind. We have moved from dealing with a painful situation and the painful response thoughts to an overall mood that is coloring our thinking. A mood that is causing the mind to react with painful thoughts to situations that may not be so painful.

Now, we pull the emergency brake on the mind. This is *mantra.*

Replacing negative thinking with *mantra* circumvents the challenge of turning the mind by finding a convincing opposite to each distressing thought. Instead, we introduce an abstract sound to change the thinking patterns that are wreaking havoc on our life.

The true opposite to any painful belief system is the vibration of love. Such is *mantra.* As we remember the *mantra*, again and again, we begin to nudge the mind from the rut of despair.

"I just can't get it right."
Om Sri Matre Namah

"It's not working anymore in this relationship."
Om Sri Matre Namah

"They don't care about me at all."
Om Sri Matre Namah

If these don't sound familiar, then rest assured that your own sample thoughts will arise spontaneously, to which you will calmly respond. *Om Sri Matre Namah. Om Namo Narayanaya. Siva Siva. Sita Ram. Babaji Babaji Babaji. Aham Brahmasmi. Tat Tvam Asi. Om Shantih.* Or anything else that comes to mind.

It might even be comforting to use a phrase in your own language. *I am loved. I am one with all beings.*

Usually, we think of *mantra* as something to be used during seated meditation. *Mantra*, however, is a transformative vibration that can calm the mind down whenever we need it: Sitting at our desk and worrying over the work to be done. During a difficult conversation with a loved one. When someone close to us is dying.

We can take refuge in *mantra* even in the simplest situations. When we've just missed the bus, again. When the grocery store is out of our favorite cereal. On the treadmill at the gym.

Whenever a thought crosses the mind that is not reflective of our natural inner joy. Whenever the mind is not at peace.

In a way, we make a sacred offering of our negative thinking. It's as if the painful idea were rice that we were tossing into the ceremonial fire, to be transformed into holy ash. *Svaha.*

Or maybe our thoughts are more like cow dung. Yes, cow dung is often used as fuel for the sacred fire.

In the *Bhagavad Gita*, Sri Krisna proclaims that He will accept whatever is offered in the light of pure devotion, be it leaf or flower, fruit or water. I've always taken this to mean that we can offer not only the best of ourselves, but also whatever else is in there. The cow dung of our minds. Our moods. Our mistakes. Our fear and anger and greed and jealousy. Our grief.

We offer these along with our hope, our faith, and our continued best effort. All will simply be received and purified by a beginningless, endless, and unconditional love.

Babaji, Immortal Yogi of the Himalayas: At a devotee's sincere request, Babaji promised never to leave his physical body, and always to remain visible to at least a few seekers on this earth. Whoever speaks his name with pure devotion will be blessed. From a painting by Peter Fich Christiansen.

It's important to realize that this way of thinking, offering the mind as if in sacred ceremony, externalizes the healing process. We also need to look deep within ourselves to awaken the truth of the heart.

So, we open to the love that heals all without question or judgement. This is why we call it unconditional. We don't do anything to deserve it. We just turn towards it.

Om Sri Matre Namah

HOW EXACTLY does *mantra* work to soothe the mind? I once attended a circus with a friend who has a small child. We bought a large bag of cotton candy to be shared between the three of us. Certainly, there was enough to go around. The plastic bag was filled with three clouds of the spun sugar. Pink, blue, and purple. Still, as we passed the bag back and forth, my friend's son became distracted from the lion tamer and the tightrope walker. He wanted more of the cotton candy.

Finally, my friend decided that he had had enough. She tucked the bag away under her seat. At this point, her son began to fidget and cry. He could no longer enjoy the show. All he wanted was the cotton candy.

Luckily, my friend had in her purse the proverbial sandwich bag full of Cheerios. This, he accepted, and we continued to enjoy the circus.

A child enjoys cotton candy just as we sometimes enjoy our ruminations. Too much sugar, however, will give anyone a bellyache. Just so, repeated thoughts of worry or blame make the mind sick. Then, we have a hard time enjoying the show, so to speak.

If we were simply to take a bag of cotton candy away from a child who is watching a circus, the child would cry. We need to replace the cotton candy with something more substantial. For a child, this might be a healthy snack, a toy, or a hand to hold.

Similarly, *mantra* replaces our unhealthy thinking patterns and gives the mind something more substantial on which to focus. It gives us a comfortable inner seat. We are then able to enjoy the great show on this earth that we call our life.

I OFFER WEEKLY MEDITATION WORKSHOPS on hospital wards for people who are suffering with afflictions of mind, like depression or addiction. I talk with them, because I know where they're coming from. I talk with them because I believe that we can all be free.

We meet at a time of great distress. One that can be a turning point in life.

Through it all, we discover the truth, together.

In these workshops, a comment that often comes up this: *Just because I stop thinking about a problem doesn't make it go away.*

These are wise words. Such an insight can lead us to liberation. Once we are able to say that there is indeed a problem, we can begin to deal with it.

The idea is not to stuff our difficulties into the suitcase of denial, slam it shut, and then lock it up with *mantra*. Emotional pain is compounded by negating the mind's reactions. We may already have been told that we are too sensitive, or that we shouldn't be feeling the way we do. That we can't be loved if we are emotional.

If we believe that our thoughts and feelings are somehow wrong, then they become difficult to move through. We might try to pretend that they don't exist, but like shadowy figures in the deep, they lurk in the unconscious mind to inform our beliefs and behaviors.

The idea that our feelings could be right or wrong raises a number of interesting questions. How can an emotion be wrong if it is an honest response? Is it more correct to lie about how we feel?

I'd say probably not. It won't be helpful in the long run to pretend that things are alright, when really, we are in pain. It's like saying that we are wearing yellow, when really, we are decked out from head to toe in blue. We can't pretend our feelings away, and we shouldn't have to try. Who is the ultimate authority on correct emotional response anyway?

When we don't get the emotional nurturing that we need, we may not know how to experience our feelings. We haven't learned by example how to accept them and to comfort ourselves. Our emotions may feel out of control, like a tidal wave or an atom bomb. As a result, we may try to shut down our emotional responses as they arise. Trying to block out our feelings can be the root of depression, addiction, or any emotional difficulty that we encounter.

A first step in healing the heart is to acknowledge our feelings as they are. We give them the attention that they deserve. As we find refuge within our own heart we can choose to embrace who we are, rather than shutting down or acting out. We learn to have an honest relationship with ourself, so that the relationship with life becomes easeful. After all, we have nothing to fear and nothing to hide.

When we face our emotions with courage and compassion, we discover that these feelings are precious. They are our teachers. Like rare jewels, they are brilliant, reflecting light from all angles. Like snowflakes falling from the sky, our emotions are delicate and unique. Opening to the beauty of our feelings allows healing to take place.

Mantra can be the refuge that allows us to open. To feel. As emotion begins to overwhelm us, we turn the mind from "me" to *mantra*. We calm down.

Mantra is the steady drumbeat of our favorite ballad. It is the candle flame that lights a room. It is the sound of the breath, like the ocean, within. It is the silence.

Eventually, the mind stops its wild leaping and bounding, its sudden veering off in disruptive directions. It grows strong enough to tolerate being with what is. It no longer needs to bring change to an external situation.

The greatest change that we can make in our lives comes from within. As we return to the refuge of *mantra* again and again, we begin to face the same challenges in life with skill and ease. The mind becomes clear and calm.

The emotional mind can be compared to a cupful of salty water. *Mantra* is like the elixir of clear water. We add fresh water to the saltwater, a drop at a time, and the bitterness is diluted. As we calmly continue to add fresh water, drop by drop, we discover that there is no longer room in the cup for both saltwater and clear water. The saltwater floods over the edge, leaving a cupful of water that is refreshing, as if it had just been drawn from a mountain spring.

Just so, as *mantra* replaces negative thinking, the bitterness is diluted. Mind heals.

Mantra awakens us to our inner radiance. When the mind is at rest, we experience the nourishing light of our own unconditional love. Like the sun, this love continues to shine throughout passing emotional storms. Eventually, it clears through the fog of our mental suffering.

This love is self-sustaining. It has neither subject nor object. It depends on nothing, and so, is limitless. Love is who we are. Beyond the cup or a cloudy sky. Beyond body and mind.

As we realize our true nature, we become aware of this same essence in all beings. We know no separation. We are an indistinguishable part of the whole. We are both in union and completely free. Suddenly, liberation in love is all there is.

Om lokah samastah sukhinoh bhavantu

May all be happy and free.

PART II:

Mantra and the Goddess

CHAPTER 1

The Birth of the Goddess

THE GODDESS appeared to liberate the world from an outrageously powerful demon. This demon was the Lord of Ignorance. Like most demons, however, he had started out as a good man. Early in life, he had been a devout spiritual seeker.

As a *sadhu*, he spent his days performing heroic austerities. He fasted from all worldly pleasures, chanted innumerable rounds of *mantra japa* on his *mala*, and spent hours in deep meditation. The gods were pleased by this. One evening as the *sadhu* sat in meditation, the gods appeared before him to offer a boon of his choosing.

The *sadhu* did not think twice. He requested rulership of the universe.

The gods hesitated. They had thought that he might ask for a kingdom or a beautiful wife, or perhaps, if he were wise, liberation. Yet the *sadhu* did not budge in his request.

The gods glanced uncomfortably at each other, knowing that they would need to be true to their word. As they had offered him a boon of his choosing, they complied with his demands. And so, the *sadhu* gained such power that he became invincible to the gods.

Unfortunately, though he gained great power through his austerities, the *sadhu's* heart was not yet pure. He had been hurt and disappointed by people he trusted, and until now, he felt that his prayers had gone unanswered. Thus, when his power manifested, he did not use it to benefit all beings.

Instead, he began to wreak havoc throughout the universe. Hailstorms came in the summertime and destroyed the crops. So, good men turned to lives of crime. They needed to put food on the table for their wives and children.

Meanwhile, their wives grew distraught and took lovers for solace. Children ceased to play, growing up too quickly in this time of trouble.

Even renunciates became confused about their purpose.

The world was falling out of balance.

The *sadhu* was intoxicated by his new power, conjuring up disaster after disaster, simply because he could. Great snakes reared up from the waters to threaten entire villages. Sacred medicinal plants withered on the mountaintops. And so, the once-devout *sadhu* became known as an *asura*, or demon.

The gods were at a loss. Such rulership of the universe could not continue. There was no question about this. Yet, this demon was now invincible to them.

They gathered on the sacred peak of Mount Meru. There assembled were Brahma the Creator, Visnu the Preserver, and Siva the Transformer. Included as well were Yama the Lord of Death and Indra the King of the Heavens. Leaving aside further discussion, the gods sat in a circle and meditated. Their powers merged.

In the center of the circle, a blazing fire appeared. The gods began to offer oblations of light, incense, rice, and flower petals. They intoned hymns from the Vedas.

The fire blazed brighter than a thousand suns.

Out of these leaping flames stepped the Goddess. She was adorned, from head to toe, with precious gemstones of every color. They glittered in the firelight.

Her smile soothed the hearts of the gods, who now trusted that the world would be alright. Although the demon had been granted invincibility to their powers, he was yet vulnerable to a woman.

The Goddess was born no ordinary woman. She was beautiful beyond imagination. Her face glowed like the full moon. Her hair was like the midnight sky. Her cheeks sparkled as rubies do, and one could only compare Her lips to freshly cut fruit. She radiated a rosy light, like sunrise.

The gods blessed Her with their every power. And so, she set off to restore the balance of the universe.

LOST IN THE VALLEY of his own darkness, the demon suddenly felt a warm and glowing light. The furrow in his brow smoothed. He looked up from his plotting and scheming to find the Goddess standing before him.

Her beauty disarmed him. As he gazed into Her eyes, the demon's mind quieted. He fell at Her feet and begged Her to marry him.

Although the demon was ardent in his desire for Her, the Goddess was wedded to love itself. Furthermore, she was fiercely independent. Each of the gods had bestowed upon Her a powerful weapon. The Goddess wielded the discus, the trident, and the bow and arrows. Behind Her stood the lion, king of all beasts, who carried Her wherever she wished to go. Her eyes radiated the strength of elephants and wild horses, even as they reflected the devotion of the gods and sages who adored Her. Gazing gently down at the demon, She commanded him to give up rulership of the universe.

The demon felt himself overflowing with bliss. His heart opened in the wellspring of Her forgiveness. Realizing the error of his ways, the demon agreed to comply with the Goddess' wishes. He gave up rulership of the universe. So, the balance of creation was restored.

THROUGH HER VARIOUS INCARNATIONS, the Goddess conquered many demons, including the buffalo demon and a pair of twin demons. Yet, though she is a fearsome warrior, she acts only out of love, to uphold righteousness and protect the universe. The most formidable demons that her love conquers are those of the mind. Feelings like lust, anger, greed, pride, jealousy, and despair.

It is said that all disturbance of mind stems from the insistence on having our way, otherwise known as attachment. When we lose or can't get what we want, we lose ourselves in the fire of emotion. Quite simply, we forget who we are.

We forget to love. We identify with emotion, which, though strong and convincing, is always passing.

Often, we act in ways that we later regret. We wreak havoc on our personal universe, creating suffering for ourselves and for those around us.

The *Sri Lalita Sahasranama* is a poem in praise of the Goddess. It is composed of a thousand *mantras.* Her thousand names.

Each name of the Goddess quiets the mind. As the mind subsides into the heart, we experience the unconditional love of the Goddess.

Her love restores us. It is a love that saves. It is also the very essence of who we are.

CHAPTER 2

The Creation of the Hymn

ACCORDING TO LEGEND, the *Sri Lalita Sahasranama* came into being at the request of the Goddess Herself.

One day, the Goddess was seated upon Her throne, where She was attended to by hosts of celestial musicians, sages, and gods. Some cooled Her with long-handled fans. Others prepared an array of confections for Her. Many took refuge at Her feet to attain enlightenment.

Radiating the light of purity and goodness, the Benevolent Mother of the Universe turned to the goddesses of speech.

"Would you compose a hymn in praise of me?" She asked.

Although She adores devotion and the sound of chanting, the Goddess did not make this request so that she might be gratified by the singing of Her praises. She is beyond the ego and its personal desires.

She made the request for the sake of those who would be chanting the hymn. Each of us. So that we could be free.

By meditating upon Her, we awaken Her essence within our own hearts.

The goddesses of speech were humbled that She had made such a request of them. They gathered to compose a pleasing hymn that would glorify Her. Each line must be unique, they thought, yet Her glories must be praised completely. Nothing can be left out.

The poetry they composed was so beautiful, that even the discarded lines enlightened those upon whose ears they fell. When they had finished, the goddesses of speech returned to the Mother of the Universe.

A hush fell over the room as all waited to hear the hymn.

The goddesses of speech began to chant. Their voices soared.

As they chanted, beautiful flowers began to bloom. Those who had been foes made peace. Many realized themselves to be love itself.

The Goddess was pleased. And so came into being this hymn that has been passed down from generation to generation. The thousand-line poem in praise of the Goddess. The *Sri Lalita Sahasranama*.

CHAPTER 3

The First Calling

WHEN I FIRST EXPERIENCED the chanting of the *Sri Lalita Sahasranama*, I thought it to be the most beautiful sound I had ever heard. It was, in fact, the first prayer that reached my ears when I landed on Indian soil.

If you've ever been to India, you know that getting there takes courage and endurance.

The trip from New York City to South India, in particular, may last twenty-one hours or three days. The length of the journey depends upon whether you calculate time passed by the clock or by your experience. If you count the number of hours to be less than a day's travel, you will yet experience, twice over, the plane's going dark as lights dim and window shades snap shut. Twice, you will nod off to the hum of the engines and awaken to the shuffling of elbows. Twice you will see the sun rise. And so, it can be said that the trip from New York City to South India lasts for three days.

After flying through Paris to Mumbai and disembarking in Kochi, I stepped into the bright stillness of the airport. It was two in the morning. I scanned the sparse crowd for the driver who was to take me the rest of the way to the *asram.*

I loaded my duffel bag into the back of a van I shared with two other travelers, a large Dutchman and a German woman with a fringed shawl tied over her jeans. Both were visiting the *asram* for the first time, as was I.

The white van bumped along the roads, churning up clouds of dust. The German woman and I covered our faces with our scarves. The air was tropical, but we were dressed for the autumn winds from which we had come. We drove for hours, passing anonymous buildings with flat white fronts, street vendors stocking their carts in the dark, and vast stretches of earth without even a coconut palm in the distance. Still, it was not yet dawn.

The van halted abruptly on the bank of the backwaters. We loaded our bags into one of the boats idling at the shore. A lithe man stood at the helm. He dipped his pole into the river, and we glided through the dark waters. Crows swooped and cawed in the mist. We unloaded on the opposite shore.

From here, we dragged our luggage through the sand. The German woman broke off from our group to find her own way. Upon reaching a courtyard, the Dutchman and I sat on our bags and waited for the main office to open. It would be some time yet before we were assigned our rooms.

We were hungry. We shared the last of our dry travel snacks.

From across the courtyard came the sound of chanting. The call was resonant. Hundreds of voices rising and falling. Sounding together, again and again.

As the chanting continued, the sky grew light.

There, sitting on my luggage at dawn, with no idea of where I would sleep that night, I thought that this might be the most incredible sound I had ever heard. Such was my first experience with the *Sri Lalita Sahasranama.*

CHANTING THE SRI LALITA SAHASRANAMA, or the *Thousand Names of the Divine Mother*, is a morning ritual for many in India. The thousand-line hymn glorifies the Goddess incarnated as Sri Lalita. The *mantras* praise Her flawless beauty, glorious deeds, divine personality, and essence of truth.

Rising before dawn to chant the *Sri Lalita Sahasranama*, one experiences the intimate stillness of morning. There is a sense of camaraderie amongst those who have risen while most still sleep, a feeling of embarking on a sacred journey as you climb the temple steps, place your cushion against the tiled floor and focus on the *arcana* book that fits into the palm of your hand.

After the hour's chanting, the world is transformed. Whereas the sky had been dark upon entering the temple, the *sadhu* walks out through the carved wooden doors to find that the sun has risen.

This appearance of light always seemed symbolic to me of the opening of the heart that comes about with the chanting of the *Sri Lalita Sahasranama.* One awakens to the light within, to the Divine Mother, who is indeed the truth of who we are.

If you are a man and think Her qualities irrelevant to you, you are mistaken. It is by surrendering to the Goddess who lives in each of our hearts that we become heroes. Where strength fails, patience triumphs. When reason falls short, intuition guides us. As conquest of desire after desire fails to satisfy, the truth within fulfills.

If you are a woman, you may learn through Her names to know yourself beyond cultural conditioning.

In the eyes of the Goddess, men and women are equal. This was one of the first teachings that I received from the *guru.*

When we awaken, we discover that there is no true distinction between male and female. We experience the light of each being as the light that is in all.

Our limitless potential is to realize that we are this brilliant source of love. When we encounter this love in action, it can awaken us. This is how I experienced my teacher. This is how we can feel the presence of the Goddess. Know Her and know yourself.

CHAPTER 4

The Mantras of the Sri Lalita Sahasranama

THE MANTRAS of the *Sri Lalita Sahasranama* bring the Goddess to life for us. They describe Her heroic feats, Her favorite foods and flowers, Her abode, and Her unimaginable beauty. Through the hymn, we come to know the Goddess intimately. Certainly, we discover Her on a physical level, but we are also privy Her thoughts and feelings, to Her very essence.

The hymn opens by describing in detail what She looks like. This makes sense. Our first impression when we meet someone is often based upon appearance.

What's different about this description of the Goddess is that Her beauty is universal. She is beyond the fads of culture or era. She is any and all of us.

The Goddess is described most often through poetic imagery, rather than specific detail. Her eyes are not deep brown or aquamarine. They are bright and expressive. Her nose is neither perfectly straight nor interesting and exotic. It resembles a budding flower. Her teeth shine like pearls. She is adorned with the sun, moon, and stars. Her form is that of the hourglass which measures time, for all time is contained in Her. Her fragrance is intoxicating. Her feet are a refuge for anyone who cares to surrender. More radiant than a thousand suns, She is reborn through our imagination, again and again.

In truth, Her beauty manifests as the world around us. The silver bark of a birch tree, a ripe persimmon, and the light of dawn are Her beauty. The sound of Her voice is in a child's laughter. A summer breeze is Her gentle touch.

As a part of the world, we too are an expression of Her beauty. Just as we are in this moment.

Realizing our natural and inborn beauty can be deeply healing during times of discontent.

A woman who was suffering from depression met, through good luck, a humble *shaman*.

For years, this woman's life had felt meaningless. Neither medication nor therapy had helped. She was resigned to the dull ache of misery, the pain of the losses she had endured.

Seeing her suffering, the *shaman* offered to sit with her for a bit. The woman agreed. She sensed that he was sincere and kind.

The *shaman* spent several hours with the woman in her small but sunny apartment. At the end of their meditation, she felt transformed. She was relaxed and smiling.

In the following months, her entire life changed. Chronic physical ailments disappeared, and she felt as though she had been reborn. It was as if none of the painful experiences in her past had ever happened. She was relieved of her sadness and met the world with renewed feelings of joy and gratitude. She attributed these transformations to the *shaman's* healing powers.

The *shaman's* friends asked him what he had done for her. He had performed no ritual, given no herbs.

The *shaman* responded that he had no special healing powers. He had simply told the woman again and again in his mind that she was beautiful.

As we realize the beauty that is our essence, we discover a new outlook on life. We engage with the world knowing that we have everything to share. We remember that we are loveable and, in fact, that we are love itself. This is the power of the beauty of the Goddess in each of us.

Reading further in the *Sri Lalita Sahasranama*, we discover the subtle attributes of the Divine Mother. The Goddess is far more than beautiful. She is of charming demeanor and flawless character. She is free of all mental agitation. She experiences neither anger nor fear. She is free from doubt. She is unselfish, and so, eternally free in action. Her mind is open and filled with bliss.

She is a role model. Never is She at a loss for how to handle life's surprises. She is wise, and she is confident. What's more, She is the wellspring of all virtue. She is patient, generous, and strong. She is loyal, for She is filled with devotion. She is anything and everything that we might hope to awaken within ourselves.

Still deeper within, Her causal essence is revealed. The Source from which body and mind are born.

Truly, the Goddess is beyond body and mind. She transcends the boundaries of the universe. She is time. She is space. And yet, she is free of both. Her being is without beginning or end. She knows no cause, for She is the cause of all. She witnesses all workings of the world that She has created. She transcends even this awareness.

She cannot be known. She can only be experienced, by one who is pure of heart.

To worship Her is not just about making offerings. It is about becoming who She is. It is about living Her ideals, and ultimately, knowing the Goddess to be who we are: beyond concept. Beyond the concept of even the Goddess Herself.

This is why the poem was written. Why we chant it.

TO NURTURE this realization, many find it helpful to focus on particular *mantras* of the hymn. We might rest our attention on the *mantra* whose meaning we would most like to experience at a particular time in our life.

Perhaps we find a *mantra* that embodies the energy of a quality that we are trying to develop in ourself. Someone who suffers from anxiety might chant *om niscintayai namah* (I bow to Her who is free from anxiety.). Someone who has difficulties with his temper might repeat *om niskrodhayai namah* (I bow to Her who does not anger.). If you wanted to nurture the seeds of generosity in yourself, you might chant *om nir-mamayai namah* (I bow to Her who knows nothing to be Her own.). These are a few simple examples. Remember, we have a thousand Sanskrit *mantras* from which to choose in the poem.

It may also be helpful to repeat the corresponding English translation softly in the mind as an affirmation.

Try clearing the mind with a particular *mantra* for a day, a week, or even longer. Whatever it takes is what's right for you.

As we replace mental or emotional disturbance with a *mantra* of the opposite quality, we loosen the hold of distress on the mind. Just as the ocean washes over a rock until it becomes smooth, so *mantra* eases our edginess. *Mantra* is gentle. It returns, as soothing and tireless as the tides, until we feel that sweet and sudden release into freedom.

AS YOU TAKE REFUGE IN THE POEM, particular *mantras* may begin to run through your mind, almost of their own accord. When you are strolling through the woods. When you are sitting at your desk. When you are on an airplane. You may find yourself repeating a *mantra* simply because you like the sound of it. The subtle assonance and alliterations. The syllables that bring the tongue to dance.

Without knowing exactly what we are chanting or why, we can let the sounds move us as they will. We can trust ourselves.

Sometimes, intuition is our best guide. It is beyond analysis. It is beyond mind. It is about living from the truth of the heart.

One of the first experiences I had with intuition and healing was through a crystal bracelet. At the time, I was a magazine journalist living in New York City. The magazines I wrote for were hip and splashy. My life, however, felt meaningless. The invitations to parties and openings did nothing to make me feel a part of the scene. After all, I was only invited because people wanted something from me: a good write-up.

My boyfriend had just broken up with me. He'd returned from a wedding in South Carolina having realized that we didn't have "what it takes." He didn't want to marry me.

Of course, I didn't want to marry him either, but being together was far better than being alone.

I felt empty inside. As usual.

I found myself wandering amongst the jewelry counters at Bloomingdale's. Perhaps a new ornament would give me a lift. If I looked good on the outside, just maybe I could feel alright for a while on the inside. As I passed the counters of glinting silver earrings and dangling chokers, I noticed a pile of bracelets in a basket. The beads were round and smooth. The colors were soft. I picked one from the bunch. The tag read "Rose Quartz: for Love and Healing."

Well, I thought, why not?

Perhaps it sounds strange, but the truth is, when I began wearing that bracelet, I started to feel better about myself and my life. The change was so noticeable that I sought out a shop that specialized in crystals.

In the Village, I discovered a haven of wooden novelties. Barely noticeable from the street, the storefront was at the bottom of a small flight of stairs. I walked down below the sidewalk to enter an expansive wonderland. Displayed there were anything from elaborately carved chess sets to raw wooden bowls.

At the back of the store was a treasure house of colored stones. Some were strung into bracelets or necklaces. Others had been polished and imprinted with animal shapes. Still others had their natural rugged face intact.

Although I could feel the power of the stones, I knew nothing about their different properties. Rose quartz might bring emotional healing, as the tag on my bracelet had truly proclaimed, but what about the stones that were deep orange, lucid purple, or shimmering white?

As I began to inquire about the uses of the different colored stones, the shopkeeper shook her head. She was wise and grounded. She saw through the image that I had so painstakingly constructed for the rest of the world. The carefully applied lip gloss. The bangs that angled across my cheekbones. The rail-thin limbs.

"Just pick up whatever catches your eye," she said gently. "You'll be drawn to what you need."

I lost myself in the delight of the smooth and glittering colors.

The store was peaceful. All wood and stone and hush. Only after I had picked out a wrist *mala*, or *mantra* bracelet, did she hand me a yellow sheet of paper that explained the healing properties of the different crystals.

Just as we may intuitively pick a crystal, so with *mantra*, we may chant whatever sound attracts the mind. Effortlessly.

We might even open the *Sri Lalita Sahasranama* at random and pick the first *mantra* that catches our eye to work with for the day, as if the book were an oracle.

As *mantra* relieves the mind's disturbance, we connect to our innate wisdom. Our natural way of kindness.

Ultimately, we experience freedom. We are released from the weight of our mental afflictions. We can lay aside the hunger of desire, as well as the angst, disappointment, and anger that are the spokes of the spinning wheel of suffering. It is not by reaching out to grasp at things that we are freed from suffering, but by moving inward to take refuge at the still point in the center.

As we purify the mind of disturbance, we realize that true being is beyond cognitive mind. The sweet divine in us cannot be understood but only experienced. Through sudden and unexplainable grace, we no longer feel isolated, or in any way separate from the rest of life. We recognize our own inner radiance. We merge with this light in all.

THIS LIGHT IS ONE with the vibration of the Sanskrit language. Sanskrit is primordial. It is everybody's mother tongue, one of the oldest known languages, so its syllables manifest great power.

When we chant the Sanskrit transliteration of the *Sri Lalita Sahasranama*, we experience the sounds of the hymn as it was originally composed. The vibration clears the cognitive mind to bring us into a state of pure being. Bare awareness.

Think of the bedroll you might pack for a camping trip. If the pillow or blanket at the center of the bedroll were rumpled, the whole thing would look out of whack. We can compare ourselves to this roll of blankets, with spirit at the center of it all, wrapped in mind that motivates the actions of the body.

As we tune into the light, or smooth the blanket at the center of the bedroll, the outer blankets of mind and body smooth out. The mind calms down, and the body heals.

Whether or not we understand the meaning of each word, the sound or subtle thought vibration of the Sanskrit transforms us.

We realize that we are simply presence, radiating light that is both immanent and transcendent.

CHAPTER 5

Nuts and Bolts

IF YOU TRULY FALL IN LOVE with the poem, you may be interested in how it's all put together, in what's beneath the initial beauty of the experience.

Paying close attention to the Sanskrit transliteration, you'll notice that the *mantras* of the *Sri Lalita Sahasranamavali* are structured in a particular way. Each line begins with the sound *om* and ends with the word *namah.*

Om is the sound of silence that underlies the fluctuations of the universe. It is the stillness that exists throughout the ongoing cycle of creation, preservation, and transformation, or the ups and downs of daily life. *Om* is the peace we find in our hearts that allows us to understand and forgive, to remain balanced during challenging times, and to enjoy all that life has to offer. Because *om* is thought to be the sound from which all created being emerged, it is a sacred beginning for each line of the poem. Each *mantra* arises from the sound current of creation.

At the end of each line, *namah* is an offering of prostrations. I bow. As we repeat this sound, it returns us to the natural state of humility and surrender. My teacher used to say that only the grass remains untouched by a hurricane, for grass is supple enough to bend and bow down to the winds. She also said that wisdom is like water; it flows down to fill the lowest places.

When we bow down, or surrender, we survive storms and receive what we need. We can relax and trust that we are moving in the right direction, into the space of the heart.

We begin to live in a state of grace. *Namah* is *om*. Surrender is bliss. And so, each *mantra* of the *Sri Lalita Sahasranamavali* rises and falls between *om* and *namah*.

THE SRI LALITA SAHASRANAMA was composed in a Vedic meter called *anustubh*. *Anustubh* is the meter of praise.

Vedic meter is characterized by the number of syllables in each line, also called a *pada*.

The word *pada* translates literally as foot. This might be the foot of a person, an animal, a pillar, or even an old-fashioned bathtub.

Pada is also used as a form of measurement. In the case of animals, old-fashioned bathtubs, and furniture like tables and chairs, we often find four feet together. Because of this phenomena in the natural world, *pada* can be used, in terms of measurement, to mean a quarter. One part of four.

When speaking of poetry, *pada* means a grouping of words. A line in a verse. Often, four *pada* come together to create a verse, also called a *sloka*. Here again, *pada* is one part of four.

Pada is the defining characteristic of meter in Sanskrit poetry. There may be four *pada* of eleven syllables in a verse, as in *tristubh*, or three *pada* of eight syllables in a verse, as in *gayatri*. The meter *anustubh*, is recognized by its four *pada* of eight syllables in a verse. It is the meter most often used in Classical Sanskrit poetry.

The *Sri Lalita Sahasranama* is often written out with two *pada* per line. In this way, the poem is chanted in couplets, with lines of sixteen syllables each. The transliteration that follows, however, is arranged in verses of four lines. Quatrains rather than a couplets. Or, with one *pada* per line. Perhaps the meter becomes apparent in this way.

The rhythm of the poem brings power and tranquility. Its meter resounds throughout the chanting of the *stotra*, or verse form. The *stotra* is traditionally chanted aloud.

THE SRI LALITA SAHASRANAMA is comprised of eleven sections. These sections appear in the *sahasranamavali*. Again, the *sahasrana-*

mavali is the litany of a thousand names in which each *mantra* is bracketed by *om* and *namah*.

Because the hymn was composed for poetic sound rather than sense, it is not divided into sections according to subject matter. The *sahasranamavali* is divided simply at every hundred *mantras*, into ten equal parts. Each part is called a *kala*.

The *Sri Lalita Sahasranama* is a part of a larger scripture, the *Brahmanda Purana*. The initial section of the poem is sometimes considered to be the story in the *Brahmanda Purana* of how the thousand *mantras* are revealed to mankind through the sage Agastya.

Agastya was a devoted disciple of Hayagriva, the horse-headed Protector of the Universe. Sitting at the feet of his *guru*, Agastya absorbed the wisdom of *mantra*, meditation, and worship. To him were revealed the sacred tales of the Goddess' incarnation and coronation, as well as the thousand names of Her attendants.

Agastya could not get enough of the teachings. He revered Hayagriva with offering after offering of kindness towards his fellow beings.

Still, one day, Agastya noticed that he had not yet heard the thousand names of the Goddess Herself.

At first, he began to tug at his beard and frown. Then, catching himself, he humbly questioned Hayagriva.

"Beloved Teacher, why is it that you have revealed to me all but these names of the Goddess Herself?"

Hayagriva gazed at him in silence. His horse's head shone, brilliant in the light of consciousness.

Agastya continued to ponder aloud. "Am I unworthy of such knowledge? Or have you simply forgotten to teach this most pivotal wisdom?"

He waited for his teacher to reply.

Still, there was no answer.

Downcast, Agastya asked, "Could it be out of neglect that you have failed to reveal Her names to me?"

When Agastya's mind had exhausted itself, Hayagriva dispelled his doubts with a single glance.

Agastya remembered all that is sacred in the relationship between *guru* and disciple. The *guru's* grace makes the disciple worthy. As such, he could not be less than fitting to receive such knowledge from his teacher. Furthermore, the *guru* is omniscient, and so, Hayagriva had forgotten nothing. Finally, the bond between *guru* and disciple is unparalleled. Never would a teacher neglect a beloved student. Thereby, Agastya was reassured. Love for Hayagriva welled up again in his heart.

Hayagriva then explained the omission. The names of the Goddess are so sacred that they can only be imparted when asked for. Such is the Vedic injunction. An exception is made for the student of great faith who has no ability to ask, either because he lacks the proper teacher, or knows not for what to ask.

"In your case, Agastya," Hayagriva said, "you have the ability to ask. You have both a teacher and knowledge of what needs to be learned. I was, therefore, awaiting your request. Now that you have asked, I will reveal all."

And so, in the clear light of consciousness, Hayagriva imparted to Agastya the *Sri Lalita Sahasranama*, for the benefit of all beings.

Such may be the first part or *kala* of the scripture.

Others consider the introductory *dhyana sloka*, a meditation on the Goddess, to be the first *kala* of the hymn. The *dhyana sloka* appears at the beginning of the translation and transliterations that follow.

Both the structure and the sense of the poem are open to interpretation. The *Sri Lalita Sahasranama* and the Goddess Herself are fascinating, because they can be understood in so many different ways.

EACH KALA of the *Sri Lalita Sahasranama* can be thought of as a vibrant flower strung onto a garland to adorn the Goddess, who is the light of the heart. The sections can also be imagined as rays of sunlight, streaming out from the heart to warm and nourish the world.

Evocative as this imagery is, the division of the hymn into sections is illusory. The essence of the entire poem is contained within each *mantra*. The infinite whole exists in the smallest part, and so, truly there can be no separate parts. Just myriad manifestations of the one truth.

What is true for each *mantra* is true for us, as well. Think of the way a full-grown tree's potential is present within a single seed. Similarly, the infinite universe exists within the heart of each created being.

Truth is an endless and vibrant expanse into which superficial differences or separations are absorbed. Life is no more or less than a string of related happenings through which it is possible to realize this underlying truth. Freedom.

To live life for the liberation of all is one way to understand spiritual practice.

Ultimately, we realize this truth within. Then, we radiate like the sun. We are unconditioned and unconditional. A source of light and love for all beings. Limitless presence.

AS WITH ANY SPIRITUAL PRACTICE, we can set whatever intention we'd like behind the chanting of the *Sri Lalita Sahasranama*. We might set the intention to purify the mind, to let go of the learned habit of responding to situations with strong emotion. We might ask for physical healing. We might wish for love, wealth, power, or peace. But we don't just want these things for ourselves. We wish everyone else to be blessed as well.

So, we can offer the chanting as a prayer both for ourselves and for others. We can include family and friends, people we know in passing, and particularly people who, through misguided efforts to find happiness, have been hurtful.

In this way, the chanting becomes an infinite blessing. We become like the Goddess, with Her many arms: Her reach extends in all directions. She can accomplish many things at once without appearing to move at all. So, too, we can bless all beings, as we make our humble offering of chanting.

We share the benefits of the poem with all beings after we rise from the cushion, as well. We let kindness be our devotion in action. Our truest offering.

As we allow life to unfold, we rest in the tender beauty of the moment. Life is love made manifest. Our lives, just as they are, are an expression of the Goddess' love for us. For all of us. The circumstances that we encounter are Her prayer for all beings to reunite with ultimate truth and be free.

As we chant the *Sri Lalita Sahasranama*, we can think of each *mantra* as a flower offered to that love without limit, to the truth of all being. A flower from the heart offered to the heart.

PART III:

The *Sri Lalita Sahasranama*

A Poetic Interpretation

i.

I THINK ONLY OF THE DIVINE MOTHER who glows with red light. Overseeing all, she wears the crescent moon that shines forth from Her crown of infinite rubies. Her smile is ever more enticing than Her shapely breasts. Both nourish the world. She sips from a jeweled cup of nectar. She glances fondly at the red lotus of long stem that blooms in the warmth of Her hand. In a pot at Her feet shines all wealth, for those whose love is true.

Let the mind rest in the lap of the Fair One who is seated upon the great lotus of silence. Her face is radiant with bliss. Her glance is gentle and sidelong. She glows with golden light and is wrapped in golden silk. In Her hand, she holds the golden lotus. She is the compassionate protectress, beautiful to gaze upon, and only to be adored. One is at peace in Her presence.

The Goddess is like a gorgeous flower to whom all swarm, as bees seek nectar. Her fragrance soothes the mind. She who holds the noose and the goad, the bow and arrows. None can resist Her charm. She is adorned with offerings of garlands and gems and *kunkum* powder of deepest red, yet She outshines these decorations, like a rose in full bloom.

She is the Great Empress, who glows with the rising light of dawn. Her eyes flood the world with compassion. She captivates with love, as She urges the seeker ever to turn within. She loves all beings as the One.

ii.

She is the benevolent Mother.
She is the reigning queen.
She rides the lion, king of all beasts.
She takes birth in the fire pit of pure consciousness.

She manifests divine purpose.
She outshines the rising of a thousand suns.
Her reach extends in all directions.
She captivates with love.
She bears the goad of anger with a benevolent smile.
She holds the mind, like a bow of blooming sugarcane, in the palm of her hand.
She directs the five senses inward, as if they were arrows.
She is like the sunrise, flooding the universe with Her reddish glow.
Her hair is intertwined with flowers.
She wears a brilliantly jeweled crown.
Her forehead glows like a half-moon.
She wears the musk smudge *bindi*, like a dark spot on the moon.
Her eyebrows arch like doorways to the shining abode of love.[1]
Her eyes dart and glint in the stream of beauty that is Her face.
Her nose is as delicate as a budding flower.
She wears a diamond nose-stud that shines like a star in the dark beauty of her face.
She fascinates Her Lord as She tucks forest flowers behind Her ears.
She wears the sun and the moon as earrings.
Her cheeks are more lustrous than rubies.
Her lips shine like freshly cut fruit.[2]
Her teeth gleam with the light of truth.
Her breath intoxicates the seeker with the scent of the fragrant betel leaf She chews.
Her voice is so melodious that one need not know the words uttered to be lost in its tones.
Her smile absorbs the mind of Siva, the Lord of liberation, in its light.
Her chin is shapely beyond compare.
She wears the marriage thread tied about her neck by the One who is beyond desire.
Her upper arms glitter with golden bangles.
Her necklace is strung with a locket of pearl, as well as myriad gemstones and crystals, all equally precious to her.

She allows Herself to be worshipped only by the One
  who truly loves.
Her breasts hang above Her navel like ripe fruit on the vine.
Her waist is barely visible.
Her abdomen has soft folds, as though a golden belt were wound
  three times around the flesh of Her belly.
She ties a scarf, red as sunrise, around Her hips.
She wears jewels and tinkling bells beneath Her skirts.
Her soft thighs have been touched only by the light.
Her ruddy knees are like crowns of precious ruby.
Her calves shine like a jeweled quiver.
Her ankles are ever hidden in modesty.
Her feet arch like the smooth back of a tortoise.
Her toenails shine with such brilliance as to enlighten all
  who take refuge at Her feet.
Her feet surpass the lotus flower as a symbol of truth.
She wears jeweled anklets, their sweet music ringing
  as the eternal *omkara* for all who surrender.
She moves with the grace of a floating swan.
Her beauty is beyond imagination.
She is robed in red silk.
Her limbs are flawless.
She glitters with all types of ornaments, worn from head to toe.
She sits in the lap of Siva, the One who has conquered desire.
She absorbs the world into silence.
Her beloved yields to Her wishes.
She lives on the central peak of Mount Meru,
  the abode of the gods.
She dwells in the heart.
She is filled with the power of all worlds and beyond.
Her palace is built of gemstone that fulfills all wishes.
She sits upon a throne of five gods, four down on bended knee
  to support the fifth, who holds her.
She lives in the great lotus forest of silence.

She dwells in a forest of flowering *kadamba* trees,
their blossoms infinite, like Her love and wisdom.
She floats on the ocean of bliss.
Her eyes entice the seeker to abandon worldly desires.
She satisfies the ultimate desire.[3]
She is the refuge for innumerable gods and sages.
She leads an army to slay Bhandasura, the demon of ignorance.
She tames the senses like a herd of wild elephants.
She commands millions of untamed horses as Her cavalry.
She wields weapons yet to be imagined, as She rides to glory
atop a nine-tiered chariot of bliss.
The sun rises and sets to please Her.
She holds death at bay.
She is the essence of fire, that of the sacrificial pit
and that of renunciation.
She gives strength to those who wage war with desire.
She is the strength and discipline of daily practice.
She delights in the dissolution of time.
She is the antidote to the seductive poisons of the world.
She uplifts those who cling to sorrow.
Her sweet glance removes all obstacles.
She takes joy in encouraging those grown tired.
She effortlessly deflects delusion.
She supports the universe with Her fingertips.
She offers delusion like grains of rice into the fire of wisdom.
She burns ignorance to blessed ash.
Her unfathomable power is praised by all.
She gives new life to love.
Her face glows with the subtle power of *mantra.*
She fulfills worldly desires,
so that the seeker may move beyond them.
She guards the dormant power of bliss.
She embodies the vibration of *mantra.*
Her subtle form contains all *mantra.*
She savors the bliss of union, as one might sip nectar.

She protects tradition.
She is of noble birth.
She rests in Her own being.
She is the crown lotus of silence.
She rises through the seven *cakras*.[4]
She loves all beings as Her children.
She resides as adoration in the heart of the seeker.
She holds inner worship to be the highest *sadhana*.[5]
She rises from the root *cakra*, the seat of basic need.

iii.

She transcends instinct and urge. 100
She rises with confidence.
She unravels the knot of the heart.
She rests in the seat of wisdom.
She breaks through the last barrier to bliss.
She rises to the thousand-petaled lotus.
She merges in a rain of nectar.
Her beauty is as blinding as a flash of lightning in the night sky.
She is ever in union.
She is the radiant power of love.
She is the rising spiral of light. 110
She is delicate yet strong, like the lotus petal.
She is the desire for divine union.
She cannot be described or imagined.
She cuts through the jungle of suffering with ease,
  as if She were a small, sharp axe.
She enjoys both material and spiritual wealth.
She is prosperity.
She blesses all who love her with abundance.
She adores devotion.
She is easily reached through devotion.
She is charmed by sincerity. 120
She protects those who love Her from all fear.
She is Mother to all who seek fulfillment.

She is praised by Sarada, the Goddess of wisdom.
She is the Mother of the earth.
She bestows worldly happiness.
She blesses the seeker with everlasting bliss.
She supports all life with Her wealth.
She can be touched only by the One beyond desire.
Her face shines like the brightest autumn moon.
Her waist is slender. 130
She is peace.
She is self-reliance.
She cannot be bound by desire.
She is not tied to action.
She remains free of impurity.
She transcends time.
She is not bound by form.
She knows no agitation.
She is free of the intertwined qualities of nature.[6]
She is indivisible. 140
She is tranquillity.
She is undisturbed by desire.
She shines in the face of disaster.
She is eternally free.
She witnesses the ongoing cycle of birth and rebirth.[7]
She creates the five elements of the physical world.[8]
She is self-sustaining.
She is forever pure.
Her wisdom transcends time and space.
She is without fault. 150
She is fulfillment.
She is without cause, for She is the cause of all.
She is sinless, and so eradicates sin.
She is beyond body and mind.
She is the Lord.
She knows no personal preference.
She churns wisdom from the seeker's desire.

She is not intoxicated by pride.
She nurtures humility.
She is free from anxiety.
She masters the ego.
She sees through the enchantment of the senses.
She cuts through delusion for those who seek truth.
She calls nothing Her own.
She roots out selfishness in the seeker.
She is ever without sin.
She brings the seeker beyond sin.
She does not anger.
She soothes the seeker's anger.
She is without greed.
She frees the seeker from the bondage of greed.
She knows no doubt.
She relieves doubt in seekers and skeptics alike.
She knows no becoming, for She is pure being.
She frees all from the changes that are the cycle of birth and death.
She is never false.
She is beyond illusion.
She knows all beings to be of Her essence.
She frees the seeker from the pain of separation.
She is indestructible.
She is unborn, and so will never die.
She is the stillness from which action arises.
She accepts with grace all that is offered,
  though She retains nothing for Herself.
She knows no equal, for She is one with all.
Her curls are dark and shining.
She is exists throughout the cycles of creation.
She does not change.
She may be difficult to attain.
She must be approached with persistence.
She is the demon-slayer called Durga.
She eradicates sorrow.

She bestows joy.
She holds no interest for those distracted by evil.
She redirects the distracted mind.
She is without harmful tendency.
She is omniscient.
She overflows with compassion.
She is indivisible, and so knows none to be equal, inferior, or superior.
She is the power of the universe.

iv.

She is the wellspring of blessings. 200
She illuminates the path of truth.
She is the Lord of all.
In Her, all exists.
She is cosmic vibration.
She is sacred symbol.
She is ritual worship.
She is consciousness.
She is married to the Lord.
She is that Supreme Being.
She takes form as the goddess Laksmi to preserve the universe and bestow prosperity. 210
She plays Her role as the beloved of Mrda.[9]
Her forms are great.
She is worshipped by all.
She uplifts those ensnared by the world.
She weaves the web of illusion.
She dispels that illusion.
She is the power of the universe.
She bestows delight beyond what is sensual.
She bestows the greatest wealth.[10]
She rules being, non-being, and beyond. 220
She is supreme strength.
She is mighty.

She is the seat of wisdom.
She manifests the power of transformation.
She is the bliss of the *yogi*.
She is ritual, the object of worship,
  and the power attained by sacrifice.
She is the sound current of creation.
She is the power of *yantra*.[11]
She is the seat of union.
She inspires sacrifice.[12]
She is worshipped by Siva, the Lord of liberation.
She bears witness to the great dance of Lord Siva,
  as he reabsorbs the universe.
She is queen to the Lord of desire.
She is the beautiful One who rules the city of light within.
She is adored in sixty-four different ways, from the washing of Her
feet to the waving of the flame, and ultimately, through the seeker's
  complete surrender.
She floods the world with the beauty of sixty-four talents,
  among them music, poetry, painting,
  and the art of polite conversation.
She draws bands of *yoginis* in the number of sixty-four crores
  to follow her example of purity.
For Her, the gods and sages have created twelve forms of worship,
  called *manuvidya*.
She is worshipped through *candravidya*,
  one of these twelve forms of worship.
She shines at the center of the moon.
She is beauty.
Her smile awakens the heart.
She wears the crescent moon in Her crown.
She loves all, the sentient and insentient, as Her creation.
She dwells in the innermost sanctum, *sricakra*.
She is Parvati, the daughter of the Himalaya Mountains.
Her eyes radiate love as they behold the world's suffering.
Her face, like a gemstone, reflects light in all directions.

She sits atop the forms of five[13] who are powerless without Her.
Her form subsumes these five.
She exists within and beyond all form.
She is supreme bliss.
She is the wisdom that illuminates mind.
She is the state of meditation, as well as the meditator
  and the object of meditation.
Her deeds express love alone,
  and so transcend right and wrong conduct.
The universe expands and contracts with Her breath.
She is the waking state.[14]
She is the dream state.[15]
She is the body of light that lives in dreams.
She is the depths of sleep.
She is the soul that merges through deep sleep.
She is witness to the states of waking, dreaming, and deep sleep.
She transcends even this state of witness consciousness.[16]
She creates the universe to watch it evolve.
She takes the form of Brahma.[17]
She protects the universe.
She takes the form of the divine child cowherd, Govinda.[18]
She allows the universe to break down.
She takes the form of Rudra[19] who brings tears, for sorrow purifies
  the heart as rain brings flowers to bloom.
She reabsorbs Her blessings,
  so that they appear to disappear.
She is Isvari, the consciousness of the universe.
She is Sada Siva, the peace of change.
She sparks the recreation of the universe.
She sustains these five functions that are the cycle of the universe.[20]
She is the light of the sun.
She dances through the fires of cremation.
She wears the six blessings[21] with humility,
  as if they were a garland of fragrant flowers.
She sits upon the lotus flower in full bloom.[22]

She looks upon all shortcomings with loving eyes.
She is like a sister.
She brings the universe in and out of being,
with the blink of her eyes.
She wears the faces of all created beings.
She has a thousand radiant eyes that are the stars, moons, suns,
and sacrificial fires.
She moves with the thousands of feet that cross the universe.
She is Mother to all beings, from the great Creator
to the earthworm at Her feet.
She structures society justly,
according to each being's innate tendencies.
Her commands are revered as scripture in the form of the Vedas.
She offers the fruit of each action in accordance with its merit
or demerit.
The red dust of Her feet decorates the foreheads of those
wise goddesses, the Vedas incarnate, who prostrate to Her.
She is the pearl of wisdom that shines from within the shell
of scripture.
She bestows the four fruits of human birth.[23]
She is forever whole, even as She brings forth the universe
from Her being.
She takes pleasure in creation.
She is both the seed of creation and the ruler of the universe.
She is the Mother of the universe.
She is without beginning or end.
She is served by the gods Brahma and Hari, who create and support
the world, as well as Indra who rules the heavens.
She takes the form of sister to Narayana,[24] He who preserves
the universe.
She is the subtle sound that pervades creation.[25]

v.

She is beyond name and form.

She utters the *mantra* that is the seed sound of creation,
preservation, and transformation: *hrim.*
She is modestly robed in Her creation,
and so known only to the pure of heart.
She rests in the hearts of all beings.
She desires no worldly pleasure,
and so knows neither attachment nor aversion.
She is worshipped by the king of kings.
She is the eternal queen.
She is delightful.
Her eyes are wide and bright like lotus flowers.
She is enchanting.
She is beloved. 310
She is the sap of bliss.
Her belt tinkles with tiny bells.
She is the soul of prosperity.
Her face is like the moon so full and bright that it shines
by the light of day.
She embodies love beyond desire.
She is the pleasure of the Lord who loves in purity.
She overcomes the army of mental demons.
She is in all aspects feminine.
She never strays from the Lord.
She is eternally desired. 320
She is the marriage of the immanent soul to its source.
She adores forest flowers.
Her holy words water the heart.
She is the seed from which the universe blooms.
She is the ocean of nectar and compassion.
From Her, the arts bud forth like figs on a tree.
Her speech is musical.
She is pure beauty.
She savors the nectar of flowers. 330
She bestows the greatest blessing.[26]
Her eyes flood the soul with silence.

She is mad with delight in the bliss of Herself.
She exists beyond the created bounds of time and space.
She can be known through the Vedas.
She rules the Vindhya Mountains,
for She has subdued their resident demons.
She offers eternal support to the universe.
She brings forth the Vedas from Her being,
as a mother births her children.
She is, at once, the truth and illusion of the universe.
She sports and plays in the world She has created. 340
She is the battlefield upon which truth conquers illusion.
She rules the field of creation.
She protects both the field of action and the one who knows it
to be illusory.
She is eternally youthful.
She is worshipped by those born into the field of play.
She knows no defeat.
She is untainted by battle.
She is only to be adored.
She knows all to be Her darling children.
She is the origin of speech. 350
Her hair is the midnight sky.
She is the light of sun, moon, and fire.
She is the flowering vine of the wishing tree.
She liberates the soul bound by animal desire.
She transforms those who have turned from truth.
She inspires all to seek the eternal.
Like moonlight, She soothes those who burn in the three fires
of purification.[27]
She is ever the fair maiden.
She is the soul of the seeker.
Her shape is like the hourglass that measures time. 360
She protects those bound by time.
She is present beyond time and space.
She lights each being from within.

She casts the illusion of many forms
over the one bliss consciousness.
Brahma is but a drop in the ocean of Her bliss.
She is the fulfillment of inner bliss.
She is unmanifested consciousness.
She is the rising of consciousness.
She is the merging of individual consciousness with the highest bliss.
She unites created being with transcendent consciousness.
She is language.
She is the swan of discrimination
that floats in the mind of the seeker.
She is the river of life in the Lord of desire.
She knows all acts of desire.
She is the object of worship for the Lord of desire.
She is ardently worshipped as the full-blown flower of love.
She is victorious over desire.
She abides in the throat of He
who swallowed the poisons of the world.[28]
She rests in the sacred seat of intuition.
She dwells in the innermost shrine of all beings.
She is the secret inner sacrifice.
She is pleased by those who seek no glory in their worship.[29]
She showers such a seeker with sudden grace.
She witnesses all workings of the worlds.
She transcends the witness consciousness.
She is One with Siva, the Lord of the six limbs.[30]
She is filled with six qualities of inner fulfillment.[31]
She is eternal compassion.
She is beyond compare.
She bestows *nirvana*.[32]
She is the essence of the sixteen eternal goddesses,
from Tripurasundari to Kamesvari.
She is consciousness that takes both male and female form.
She is the light that pervades all.
Her form is luminous.

She is revered.
She is the supreme ruler.
She is the root cause of all that manifests in the natural world.
She is the imperishable unmanifest that supports the natural world.
She is the union of the manifest and unmanifest.

vi.

She pervades all. 400
She takes innumerable forms.
She is both wisdom and ignorance.
She is like a water lily shining in the moonlight of the Lord's gaze.
Her affections are like sunlight,
  dispelling the shadows of ignorance in all hearts.
Transformation is her herald.
She is worshipped by the Lord of liberation.
She is the form of that Lord of liberation.
She confers the bliss of liberation.
She is adored by the Lord of liberation.
She transcends liberation. 410
She is beloved to the wise.
She is worshipped by those who renounce the pleasures
  of the world.
Her love is immeasurable.
She is lit from within.
She absorbs thought and speech.
She is the power of pure consciousness.
She is consciousness made manifest.
She is the workings of natural law.
She is the soul of inanimate being.
She is the one who saves. 420
She is the utterance of *mantra*.
She is the object of meditation.
She is to be adored at twilight.[33]
She rests upon the subtle forces of the world.
She supports the physical world.

She is transcendent reality and its appearance as created being.
To Her, the soul cries out for union.
She is the five veils of the soul.
She transcends ideas of body, mind, and bliss.
She is the wellspring of youth and beauty. 430
She is in ecstasy beyond the worlds.
Her eyes roll upward with pleasure.
Her face is flushed with bliss.
Her limbs are adorned with fragrant sandalwood paste.
She is fond of the budding flowers at her feet.
She is skillful in all aspects of creation.
She acts with grace throughout creation.
She leads the seeker from the desires of ego to pure consciousness.
She rules the river of consciousness as it flows ever upward.[34]
She is seated at the source of this river. 440
She is worshipped by all who are selfless.
She is mother to those bound by the illusion of separation.
She is contentment.
She is the ripe and perfect fullness of being.
She is wisdom.
She is strength.
She is serenity.
She absolves the seeker from sin.
She is the source of all light.
She is joy. 450
She clears the path of obstacles.
She is the inner light of creation.
She sees all with the inner eye.[35]
She is all that is desired in a woman.
She is garlanded as the One beyond bodily form.
She is the great *mantra* of the breath: *so'ham hansah.*
She breathes life into all beings.
She dwells amongst the sandalwood groves of the Malaya Mountain.
Her face is sweet.
Her limbs are as soft as lotus petals. 460

Her eyebrows are pleasingly arched.
She is the source of all beauty.
She leads the gods.
She is the sole refuge for the Lord.
Her beauty is brilliant.
Her loveliness agitates the mind.
Her form is subtle.
She is the thunder in the heavens.
She is to be worshipped.
She knows neither childhood nor old age,
for Her heart is ever in the bloom of youth. 470
She has all powers at her command.
She knows the greatest power to be knowledge.
She brings forth all power from Her being.
She is famed throughout the worlds that come in and out of being.
She resides in the throat *cakra* as the goddess Dakini.
As Dakini, She has a complexion of rosy bloom.
As Dakini, she is three-eyed, and so, all-seeing.
As Dakini, She bears a club to eradicate the ego.
As Dakini, Her face radiates the light of transformation.
As Dakini, She is fond of sweet milk pudding. 480
As Dakini, She is the goddess of touch.
As Dakini, She is frightening to those who fear their own potential.
As Dakini, She rests in the sixteen-petaled lotus of the throat
and is attended to by sixteen goddesses.
She is the goddess Dakini, the purified mind that dances
in the limitless space of consciousness.
She resides in the heart *cakra* as the goddess Rakini.
As Rakini, She is black in color.
As Rakini, She offers two faces to the world,
casting the illusion of duality.
As Rakini, She has gleaming tusks.
As Rakini, She wears Her weapon, the discus, strung on a necklace.
As Rakini, She is bloodthirsty in Her slaying of the ego. 490

As Rakini, She stands at the center of the twelve-petaled lotus,
where twelve attendants await Her commands.
As Rakini, She savors clarified butter whenever it is offered.
As Rakini, She is the strength of heroes.
She is the ever-benevolent Mother in the form of Rakini.
She resides in the center of power, behind the navel,
as the goddess Lakini.
As Lakini, She shows the world three faces, in the spirit of creation,
preservation, and transformation.
As Lakini, She holds the dart, the thunderbolt, and the discus.
As Lakini, She sits in the center of the ten-petaled lotus
with Her ten attendants.
As Lakini, She is the color of life blood.

vii.

As Lakini, She rules the transformation and desire
of the flesh. 500
As Lakini, She is delighted by confections.
As Lakini, She bestows sweet joy upon those who worship Her.
She is the One Mother in the form of Lakini.
She resides in the *cakra* of creation as the One who is called Kakini.
As Kakini, She fascinates with Her faces that are four,
like the fruits of human birth.
As Kakini, She bears the trident as her weapon, along with the noose
of binding love and the skull of the slain ego.
As Kakini, She shines with a golden hue.
As Kakini, She is dignified, strong, and beautiful.
As Kakini, She is the ruler of excess.
As Kakini, She adores offerings of dripping honey. 510
As Kakini, She is attended by six,
as She rules from the six-petaled lotus.
As Kakini, She cools Her food with curd.
She is the essence of the form called Kakini.
She rises from the root *cakra* as the goddess Sakini.
As Sakini, She has five faces, reflecting the five elements.

As Sakini, She rules inner structure.
As Sakini, She holds the elephant goad, the lotus, a book,
  and *jnana mudra*, the seal of wisdom.
As Sakini, She is served by four,
  from Her seat of the four-petaled lotus.
As Sakini, She savors the taste of *mudga* beans.
She is the Mother in the form of Sakini. 520
She resides in the seat of intuition, between the eyebrows,
  as the goddess Hakini.
As Hakini, She is pure white in color.
As Hakini, Her faces are six, like the senses.[36]
As Hakini, She manifests as the innermost essence of form.
As Hakini, She keeps two favored attendants by her side,
  as She sits upon the two-petaled lotus.
As Hakini, She adores the taste and fragrance of saffron.
She takes the form of Hakini.
She lives in the eternal silence of the thousand-petaled lotus,
  as the goddess Yakini.
As Yakini, She is resplendent, for She shines with all colors.
As Yakini, She holds weapons yet to be imagined
  in each of Her thousand hands. 530
As Yakini, She is the source of creation.
As Yakini, She sees in all directions.[37]
As Yakini, She finds all food delectable,
  for She is beyond preference.
She is the Mother in the form of Yakini.
She is Vedic sacrifice, as well as the call of offering: *svaha*.[38]
She is the gift that satisfies the spirit: *svadha*.[39]
She exists before the dawn of knowledge.
She is the intelligence incipient in ignorance.
She is the song of scripture.
She is the remembrance of truth. 540
Her heart floods the universe with wisdom.
Her blessings are glorious.
She is known through the purity of Her deeds.

Her name brings purity when sung in praise.
She is worshipped as the One who upholds the heavens.
She frees all from the prison of impure deeds.
Her dark locks flow down her back in waves.
She is the first vibration of light.
She is the power to know the real from the unreal.
She is the infinite love from which all beings are born. 550
She calms fears of illness and aging.
She lives beyond death.
She is the first cause of all.
Her form outlasts the thinking mind.
She purifies the Iron Age of sin, as light dispels darkness.[40]
She is the essence of light.
In Her gaze, time is stilled.
She is worshipped by the lotus-eyed One.
Her mouth is full of betel leaf.
Her face is as bright as the pomegranate flower. 560
Her eyes are like a fawn's.
Her beauty silences the mind.
She is a natural leader.
Her rule gives happiness.
She is a friend to all.
She is eternal contentment.
She fulfills longing.
She is inner guidance.
She rules all that is, all that is not, and all that will come to be.
She brings peace of mind through Her friendship. 570
She dances with the Lord, and the universe is absorbed.
She is the power that underlies creation and dissolution.
She is the dissolution of ignorance.
She is the form of pure knowledge.
Her limbs are as languid as the drunk's.
She is intoxicated by the wine of the heart.
She births the alphabet in a single breath.

She abides in the ether that floats above Mount Kailas,
 home to Lord Siva.
Her arms are as graceful as flowering vines.
She is adored. 580
She embodies mercy.
She rules the universe sweetly,
 as if She were the mistress of a modest home.
She is the knowledge of the soul.
She is devotion.
She is the great Goddess *mantra*, the *srividya* of fifteen syllables
 that bestows the fruit of all *mantra*.[41]
She is adored by the formless Lord.
She is the truth of the *srividya mantra*,
 made sixteen-syllabled for the pure seeker.[42]
She is the three parts of that same Goddess *mantra*:
 body, mind, and soul.
She frees the seeker from these three modes of bondage.
She is attended by hosts of goddesses, those bestowing
 all prosperity, who bow at her very glance. 590
She is ever in the state of meditation.
She is the calm light of the moon.
She adorns the seeker's forehead as the *bindu*
 of the sacred syllable *hrim*.
She shines with all colors of the rainbow.
Her abode is the heart.
Her love is self-sustaining, like sunlight.
She is the flame that lights the three worlds.[43]
She is the One for whom the stars shine.
She eradicates impurity.

viii.

Her love is the sacrificial fire. 600
Her gentle gaze dispels fear.
She lights the world with Her smile.
She removes darkness.

She is the merciful ocean that dissolves suffering.
She is Mother to the sacred cow.
Her offspring overcome all obstacles.
She is Lord of the gods.
She rules fairly.
She is the subtle Self.
She is worshipped with the phases of the moon,
from new to full. 610
She is all phases of the moon's cycle.
She is the cycle of birth and death.
She delights in poetry.
To Her, the goddesses of prosperity and wisdom tend,
with long-handled fans.[44]
She is the primal energy of the universe.
Her being knows no bounds.
She is the truth in all.
She is supreme being.
She is purity.
She births infinite worlds. 620
She is of divine form.
She is the sacred seed sound of desire: *klim*.
She desires nothing, for She is inherently complete.
She renounces the world, though she moves within it.
She bestows absolute bliss.
She rules all modes of trinity.[45]
She is the merging of the mind with the heart.
She is all that is worshipped.
She rules all forms of divinity.
She is the desire that yields to wisdom. 630
She is of divine fragrance.
She wears the mark of vermilion, like a rising sun on her forehead.
She is as delicate as a China rose.
She is the mountain princess.
She glows with a golden hue.
She inspires the songs of angels.

She births the universe from a golden egg.
She births all from Her shining womb.
She defeats demons.
She presides over speech. 640
She is known when the mind is quiet.
She transcends space and time.
She grants wisdom beyond intelligence.
She is true knowledge.
She is the One whom the scriptures praise.
She is the blissful source of truth.
She is worshipped by women whose hearts are pure.
She births and reabsorbs Her worlds, as if it were child's play.
She is the seer behind the eyes.
She transcends all that the eyes can see. 650
She knows all that is to be known.
She transcends the knowledge of mind.
She is ever in union.
She bestows union upon the seeker.
She is the union of body, mind, and soul with pure consciousness.
She is the bliss of union.
She is the love that unites myriad created beings as one.
She is the power of desire, tempered by wisdom,
  and offered as purity in action.
She is one with creation.
She is firmly rooted. 660
She underlies manifest and unmanifest existence.
Her forms are eight, like the limbs of *yoga*.[46]
She dispels illusion.
At Her will, the worlds come in and out of existence.
She is unity.
She is the past, present, future, and that which is unmanifest.
She is beyond the duality of the manifest and unmanifest.
She dissolves duality.
She feeds the world.
She bestows prosperity. 670

She is the primordial giver of life.
She is the merging of form with no form.
She is vast.
Her wisdom is like a healing herb:
  the antidote to the suffering of ignorance.
She is wedded to love itself.
She is the ecstasy of union.
She adores offerings of true love.
She is the honeyed tone of the lover's voice.
She commands powerful forces.
She neither is nor is not. 680
She brings no suffering to those who love her.
She blesses those who err.
Her holy footsteps are easy to follow.
She rules great monarchs.
She bestows the crown of wisdom.
She is beloved by those who rule.
She rules with compassion.
She raises servants to be kings.
She is the wealth of kings.
She parts the five veils of the soul,
  so that the soul may merge with truth. 690
She leads the world's armies,
  complete with cavalry, infantry, chariots, and elephants.
She bestows dominion in the three worlds and beyond.
She is one with truth.
She is Mother Earth, who wears the ocean as Her girdle.
She lives under holy vow.
She soothes the mind that is agitated by desire.
Her charm calms the three worlds.
She grants all wishes.
She creates all that is desired.

ix.

She is the form of truth, consciousness, and bliss. 700

She is space.
She is omnipresent.
She enchants all.
She is Sarasvati, the Goddess of wisdom.
From Her, the sciences flow.
She lights the cave of the heart.
She is the essence that is imperceptible to the senses.
She is free from the illusion of separation.
She is devoted to the silence.
She is the wisdom that is transmitted through silence. 710
She purifies.
She is the all-pervasive teaching.
She is the inner circle of devotees.
She breaks the bondage of sensory pleasure.
She is adored as the sun disc.
She is the power of illusion.
Her glance is like wild honey.
She manifests the illusion of the world.
She is Mother to truth-seekers.
To Her, the gods bow. 720
Her limbs are soft.
She is the beloved of the *guru* who removes the shadows of ignorance.
She creates all from within Herself.
She brings forth the wisdom of the Lord.
She takes form as the Lord to instruct the gods.
She is worshipped by a succession of *gurus.*
She bestows the wisdom of silence.
She is consciousness come to live in the world.
She is the budding flower of bliss.
She is pure love. 730
She arouses feelings of devotion.
She takes pleasure in the chanting of Her many names.
She is the power of wisdom.
She rules the dance of life.

She upholds the worlds that come in and out of existence.
She bestows liberation.
She is liberation in female form.
She adores the dance of life.
She is the hush of beauty.
She is modest. 740
She is feminine.
She douses the fires of worldly desire in a rain of nectar.
She is the forest fire of purification.
She is the breeze that blows misfortune away.
She is like sunlight, dispelling the shadows of affliction.
She is the moonlight reflected in the ocean of bliss.
She is the rain cloud complexion of the Beloved
  who brings the peacocks to dance.[47]
She is the thunderbolt that splits the mountain of sorrow.
She is the axe that cuts the tree of suffering.
She is the great Goddess. 750
She rules fate.
In time, She devours all.
She consumes the universe.
She liberates all from their debts of past action.[48]
Her mercy inspires awe.
She calms the demons of lust and anger.
She is both perishable and imperishable.
She rules all worlds.
She supports the universe.
She creates the play of ignorance, passion, and goodness. 760
She is all worldly blessing.
She sees all that exists, throughout the worlds and within each being.
She is the balance of nature that brings freedom.
She bestows the merits of heavenly birth.
She is pure.
She is like a flower petal, offered to the sacred fire of purification.
She is the power of desire turned inward.
She is the torchbearer of spirituality.

She is a living sacrifice.
She adores vows of any kind,
  be they those of marriage or renunciation. 770
She is to be worshipped consistently.
She responds to the cry of surrender.
She is easily pleased by offerings of trumpet flowers,
  from which She sips nectar.
Her greatness cannot be fathomed by the mind.
She lives on the mountain that is home to the gods.
She adores the blossoms of the coral tree.
She is the beloved of heroes.
She is the power of the universe.
She is steadfast.
She faces outward in all directions. 780
She is the innermost essence.
She is the ever present space.
She gives life to all beings.
She is breath.
For Her, the glorious sun rises.
Her mind is absorbed by the chanting of *mantra.*
She harmonizes the realms of body, mind, and spirit.
Her army brings everlasting peace.
She is devoid of nature's passions.
She lives within and beyond the natural world. 790
She is truth, bliss, and wisdom come to life.
She is fond of the songs of truth.
Her body is sanctified by the matted locks of Lord Siva.
She wears a garland of beauty and brilliance.
She fulfills all desire.
She is the essence of desire.
She is the ocean of inspiration.
She adores poetry.
She is the subtle beauty of the arts.

x.

She is the wellspring of nectar. 800
She is well-nourished.
She is most ancient.
She is worshipped by all.
She is as fresh as the lotus blossom.
Her eyes dance with music.
She is the light behind all light.
She is the sole refuge.
She is the space within the atom and beyond the universe.
She transcends the changing lights of dawn and dusk.
She holds the noose of worldly love. 810
She liberates all beings from worldly bondage.
She breaks the spell of the world's enchantment.
She is the illusion of form.
She is the formless divine.
She is contented amidst the changes of the universe.[49]
She knows ultimate truth in the impermanent world.[50]
Truth is Her beloved.
She is truth.
She is the essence of created being.
She is faithful to creation. 820
She gives life to creation.
She is the truth of creation.
She is the Mother of all beings.
She is of myriad forms.
She is worshipped by the wise who seek the truth of unity.
She creates all, from earth to ether, and beyond.
She feigns wrath to preserve righteousness.
Her law brings liberation.
She is the foundation of the world.
She experiences Herself in all beings. 830
She reins in the senses as if they were wild horses.
She pleases the senses.
She is the eternal wreath of letters.[51]

She is untainted by action.
She is ever holy.
She births heroes.
She is the primordial ether.
She is the most precious jewel.
In Her, bliss resides.
She is the taproot of life. 840
She is the wisdom of being.
She remedies the pain of birth and rebirth.
She turns the wheel of suffering.[52]
She is the steady worship that yields wisdom.
She is the thread of wisdom.
She is the source of *mantra*.
Her waist is slender,
  like a graceful bridge from desire to consciousness.
She is known to all.
Her glories are limitless.
She is the breath of the spoken word. 850
She lends solace to those near death.
She is praised throughout the Upanisads.
She is the essence of peace.
Her depths are endless.
She rests in space.
She raises each being as Her own child.
She sings with abandon.
She calms the crashing waves of the mind.
She is the supreme goal.
She is the end of all pain. 860
She is ever merged in love with the Lord.
She is untouched by cause and effect.
She is the overflowing river of pleasure.
She wears shining golden earrings.
She takes form only to play.
She is ever unborn.
She is free in form.

She infatuates all.
She is easily pleased.
She can be known by looking into the heart. 870
She eludes those distracted by the world.
She is the source of the Vedas.
She is all time.
She pervades all as the eternal *omkara*.
She rules the three cities of body, mind, and soul.
She is free of illness.
She depends on nothing, and so, supports the universe.
She delights in the bliss within.
She is the stream that floods the world with bliss.
She rescues those who are caught in the current
of illusion. 880
She adores sacrifice.
She performs all sacrifice.
She receives all sacrifice.
She supports righteousness.
She is the treasure house of material and spiritual wealth.
She bestows gold and grain.
She is beloved to the wise.
She gives the sage his second birth.[53]
She turns the world.
She absorbs the universe in the depths of Her belly. 890
She is the fire of renunciation.
She is the eternal refuge.
She takes form to uplift the world.
She is unborn.
She is the source of creation.
She stands strong in the face of ignorance.
She is the distant shore of freedom.
For Her, heroes fight.
She is valour.

xi.

She is the peace that calms all struggle.
She is the shimmer of cosmic sound.
She is the wisdom of the heart.
She is the elixir of light.
She is artful creation.
She rests in changeless being.
She is the essence of the elements.
She is the truth of the natural world.
She brings to life the *mahavakya*, "Thou art That."[54]
She listens joyfully to the chanting of Vedic hymns.
She is as gentle as moonlight.
She is wedded to silence.
She is the subtle balance between effort and grace.
She lights the path like a delicate lamp.
She is fiercely independent.
She is slow and sweet, like honey.
She reveals all to be one.
She is revered by those who have realized truth.
The wise offer Her their minds, as one offers rice into the sacrificial fire.
She is the nectar deep within the flower of consciousness.
She is sublime.
She is eternally pleased.
Her light is as soft and rosy as the dawn's.
She accepts all that is thought, said, or done as sacred offering.
Her face glows like the shining hollow of a conch shell.
She stills the pendulum that swings from aversion to desire.
Her love cannot be bought.
She revels in the blessings that pass between beings.
She receives all praise.
She is praised throughout the scriptures for Her mastery of mind.
She is the workings of the mind.
She calms the emotional mind, so that wisdom shines forth.
She is the child empress of the universe.

Her every deed is a blessing to the world.
She is the Mother of the universe.
She supports all creation.
Her eyes are large and luminous.
She is impartial.
She is bold.
She is infinitely giving.
She is ever joyful. 940
Her mind contains all mind.
Her hair is the sky above.
She rides the chariot of light.
She wields the lightning bolt.
She is the Goddess to whom the wise offer their lives in sacrifice.
She is Beloved to those who perform the five rituals of sacrifice.[55]
She reclines on a sofa of five gods, four who kneel as the legs to support the fifth, with whom She is ever in union.
Her love is sacred.
She wears a sparkling necklace strung from the gems of the elements: the emerald of earth, the pearl of water, the ruby of fire, the diamond of air, and the sapphire of ether.
She is worshipped five times over with sweet pudding, flower petals, light, incense, and holy water. 950
She is eternally worshipped.
She rules eternity.
She bestows joy.
She enchants the Lord.
She brings forth the wilderness.
She is the daughter of the mountain king.
She is all wealth.
She is righteousness.
She waters seeds of righteousness in the heart.
She transcends heaven and earth. 960
She commands the forces of nature.
She is both intimate and everywhere.
She is soothing.

She is vibrant, like the red bloom of the *bandhuka* flower.
She plays like a child.
She delights in the workings of the universe.
She brings about immeasurable fortune.
She bestows sweet blessings.
She is draped in silk.
Her love is undying. 970
She is pleased when a husband worships his wife.
Her beauty shines throughout the world.
Her mind is pure.
She is deeply satisfied with whatever is offered.
She is the cause of intelligent life.
She lives beyond form.
She is worshipped with ten *mudras*.[56]
She is the benevolence of truth.
She is *jnana mudra*.[57]
She dotes on those who seek wisdom. 980
She is all that is to be known, as well as the path to that knowledge.
She uplifts those who have fallen along the path.
She rules the lower, middle, and upper worlds.
She balances the three qualities of nature.
She is the gentle Mother.
She is the triangle of creation: birth, maturation, and dissolution.
She knows no pain in Her created worlds.
She protects Her creation fearlessly.
She spoils all beings with the wealth of love.
She can be known easily through discipline. 990
She is the essence of all that is worshipped.
She overflows with compassion.
She dispels the shadows of suffering.
She can be known by all.
Intimacy with Her brings the seeker to his knees.
She dwells at the center.
She is the blessed Mother who rules in beauty.
She is absolute bliss.

She is eternal union.
She is who I am: I bow again and again to this light in all.

Notes

[1] Her eyes.

[2] Or polished coral.

[3] The ultimate desire is that for liberation. This desire to be enlightened overcomes all other desires. It is like the soap rubbed into a stained cloth. When the soap and the dirt are both washed out, then the cloth is clean.

The enlightened one lives completely free of desire. She realizes that she is one with all. Her consciousness is all consciousness.

Until we awaken to this truth, we may desire enlightenment not only for the sake of ourself but also for the sake of all beings, that they too may be awakened and free from suffering. This desire is the soap that is rubbed into the stained cloth and then washed out.

Once we are liberated, there is no further desire. We are presence, without condition or limit.

[4] The *cakras* are seven subtle energy centers that lie along the midline of the upper body. From the base of the spine to the crown of the head, they are the *muladhara cakra*, the *svadisthana cakra*, the *manipura cakra*, the *anahata cakra*, the *visuddhi cakra*, the *ajna cakra*, and the *sahasrara cakra.*

Each *cakra* is said to be the source of energy for a different area of life. Their associated seed sounds, or *bija mantras*, are Lam, Vam, Ram, Yam, Ham, Om. These six sounds can be chanted to clear obstacles in daily life and realize meditative bliss through the silence of the *sahasrara cakra.*

[5] *Sadhana* is spiritual discipline. This may be a formalized course of study, ritual, or service, or any action that is an offering. The

particular action itself is less important than the intention behind it. Household chores or an office job can be *sadhana* when we see the work as an offering, or a path to freedom.

Of course, finding time for study and meditation are important to keep the focus on selflessness rather than on worldly gain.

[6] The qualities of nature are called the *gunas*. They are *tamas*, *rajas*, and *sattva*, or ignorance, passion, and goodness. Passionate desire overcomes the lethargy of ignorance. The wish to be good overcomes selfish desire.

Ultimately, the seeker acts in the world without personal motivation. Not even the desire to be good. So, she benefits all beings. Effortlessly.

[7] Birth, maturation, death, and rebirth.

[8] The five elements are earth, water, fire, air, and space. Each element is associated with one of the bodily senses or organs. Earth relates to the sense of smell and to the nose. Water is associated with the sense of taste and with the tongue. Fire is linked to the sense of sight and to the eye. Air implies the sense of touch and the skin. Space corresponds to the sense of hearing and to the ear.

The sensory experience associated with each element is considered to be the subtle form of that element. The subtle forms of the elements are called the *tanmatras*. Sensory experience is then perceived by mind and conceptualized by personality and intellect.

The personal experience with the elements, or with the world around us, can also be understood through Buddhist philosophy as the interaction of the five aggregates: forms of the perceiver and perceived, perception, sensation, reaction, and of course, the consciousness that allows all experience to take place.

[9] A name for Lord Siva.

[10] The wise consider the greatest wealth to be non-material. Perhaps it is love or wisdom. Ultimately, it is enlightenment. Enlightenment is an endless gift to be shared with all.

[11] A *yantra* is a sacred geometric symbol. A *yantra* may represent anything from planetary energy to a deity. The Sri Yantra is said to represent the Goddess, the merging of form with the formless, or absolute union.

[12] The greatest sacrifice is the offering of ourself to the fires of devotion, service, and wisdom. When we act out of love or compassion for all beings, this is no sacrifice.

The *Candogya Upanisad* describes life as a sacred ritual. As we go about our day, the sky is the altar, the sun is the sacred fire, and our actions are the oblations. So, we live our lives as an offering to all.

[13] These five may be thought of as gods, elements, senses, or sheaths of the soul.

The five sheaths of the soul are the *annamaya kosa* or the physical body, the *pranamaya kosa* or the energy body, the *manomaya kosa* or the mind, the *vijnanamaya kosa* or wisdom, and the *anandamaya kosa* or the bliss body. The *annamaya kosa* is maintained by food. The *pranamaya kosa* is related to the breath, as well as to action. It is purified by conscious breathing, as well as kind deeds. The *manomaya kosa* is shaped by thought. The *vijnanamaya kosa* is purified through study and contemplation. The *anandamaya kosa* may be experienced through meditation.

All that we take in, on a physical or subtle level, affects the five bodies. Just as the food we eat affects the health of the physical body, so conversation, books, films, thought, and spiritual practice affect our connection to consciousness. We are mindful of the *ahara*, or that which we take in.

These five may also be understood, according to Sankhya philosophy, as the states through which consciousness rises: body or sense perception, mind, ego, wisdom, and bliss.

Awareness begins with the body's sensory experience. It then rises to simple mind understanding, or identification of sensation. From mental cognition awareness moves through egoic preference. Like and dislike are then tempered by wisdom. Through wisdom we realize soul consciousness. Initially, the awakened one may distinguish between *prakrti* and *purusa*, or the natural world and formless bliss. Ultimately, we experience nondualism.

Beyond individual soul consciousness sits the Goddess. She experiences no division or limit. For Her, the world within merges with the created world. This is the state of union.

Both Sankhya philosophy and the Upanisads refer to this all-pervasive union as Brahman. We may also call it *samadhi*, *nirvana*, *satori*, God, or the Great Spirit.

Truly, this experience is beyond name or form, cause or concept.

[14] Sensory experience.

[15] Subtle experience.

[16] The four states of consciousness are said to be waking, or *jagrat*, dreaming, or *svapna*, deep sleep, or *susupti*, and the awakened witness of the first three, or *turiya*. The Goddess transcends these states, for She is beyond consciousness itself.

[17] In the Hindu trinity, Brahma is the power of creation. Visnu is the force of preservation or balance. Siva is the energy of destruction or transformation.

Siva is not associated with nihilistic destruction; whatever ends ends so that we can begin something new. Siva is also the great meditator, one who is attached to nothing, the silence, and the liberating power of the universe.

[18] Govinda is a name for Sri Krisna, an incarnation of Visnu. Govinda refers to Krisna in his youth, when He was a cowherd. Just as He guided and protected the cows, so metaphorically, He

supports, guides, and protects all beings, as we return to the source from which all experience arises.

[19] An incarnation of Siva.

[20] The cycle of the universe includes creation, preservation, dissolution, absorption, and recreation.

[21] The six great blessings are often named as love, valour, generosity, beauty, wisdom, and influence. They are open to interpretation and may be named differently.

[22] The lotus flower is a symbol of liberation. This flower grows up from the mud at the bottom of rivers. It is, in fact, nourished by this mud, or muck.

Just so, we may be fortified by the challenges we face. A difficult situation is an opportunity for growth. We can learn how to handle changing circumstances in a more effective way. We can expand beyond our ideas of who we are and what we think we need to be happy.

The lotus is also legendary for its bloom. Its petals are sacred in that anything that falls onto them rolls right off of them. The bloom remains pure and untouched. Similarly, we can learn to live in such a way that we rest undisturbed by anything that comes our way.

The lotus flower is also inspirational in that it floats upon the surface of the water. It is said to be in the water but not of the water. Just so, the wise one acts in the world but is not of the world. The liberated soul may participate in worldly life, while remaining completely free of desire and attachment. She simply does what needs to be done for the liberation of any and all beings.

[23] The four fruits of human birth are *ardha*, *kama*, *dharma*, and *moksa*. They are wealth, pleasure, virtue, and liberation.

Wealth and pleasure may be experienced through *tantra*. We enjoy the gifts of the world as an expression of divine grace and truth. We then give back, offering all that we receive as a form of worship.

Abundance and pleasure are positive. They balance our disciplined efforts. They allow us to feel playful.

That said, on a relative level, attachment to material wealth or pleasure often brings something else. Suffering. We suffer when we cannot get what we want in the way that we want it. So, we begin to explore wealth and pleasure in a way that is more subtle.

Wealth and pleasure can be nonmaterial. We might consider wealth to be the luxury of time, or an abundance to be shared. The greatest wealth is often said to be wisdom.

Meanwhile, pleasure can be experienced in a subtle way as well. We expand beyond the obvious bodily or sense pleasure to appreciate more lasting joys: Meditative bliss. Infinite altruism.

Our ideas of wealth and pleasure evolve as our understanding grows. With discriminative awareness, we can let go of attachment to material wealth and pleasure, and live according to the *dharma*. We can live in kindness. We can live in virtue.

Living selflessly leads to *moksa*. *Moksa* is the culmination of all birth and experience. It is liberation.

[24] Narayani.

[25] The sound of *om*. Also called *nadam*, the unstruck sound.

[26] Enlightenment.

[27] Fire purifies a precious metal like gold, causing all impurities to be released. So, three fires purify the mind. These are the fires of *karma* (the natural law of cause and effect), desire, and austerity.

The fire of desire is a yearning for something impermanent that cannot bring lasting fulfillment. In contrast, austerity is the burning renunciation of worldly attachments for realization of the truth within.

When we realize that our unending desires cannot be fulfilled, the blaze of desire yields to the purifying flame of renunciation. Through austerity, we become free from the cycle of *karma*, or action that is motivated by personal interest.

Renunciation does not necessarily mean classical asceticism, though this is a powerful and direct road to freedom.

The *Bhagavad Gita* explains austerity also as renunciation in action, or selfless service. We may live in the world and act for the well-being of all. This is renunciation in the same way that retreating to a forest or an *asram* to give up worldly life might be.

The great saint Bhagavan Sri Ramana Maharshi named austerity, *tapas*, as inquiry into the source of our personal identity, or our ideas of individual self. From where does this notion of "I" arise?

Whether we retreat, offer service, or simply inquire, austerity does not imply suffering. The only thing we are giving up is that which causes suffering. Renunciation yields complete freedom.

[28] Nilakantha is a name for Siva. This name refers to his blue throat. The *Srimad Bhagavatam* tells the story of how the gods churn the milk ocean into one of nectar. As they churn, poisons begin to spew up. Siva swallows these poisons, so that no one will be harmed. As such, His throat turns blue.

The point is that Siva is impervious to the poisons of the world. To illustrate this quality, he is often depicted as wearing a poisonous snake as an ornament around his neck.

It's interesting to note that in Buddhist philosophy the three worldly poisons are named as attachment, aversion, and ignorance. The respective antidotes are meditation, patience, and wisdom.

[29] When we worship from the heart, we need no wordly adulations. Devotion is its own reward, as is the bountiful grace of the Lord that flows towards the sincere devotee.

Such a seeker may offer oblations in a solitary place, or pure deeds into the fire of the heart. This seeker may appear to be a completely ordinary person who quietly lives daily life as an offering.

[30] The six limbs may be known as strength, contentment, independence, wisdom, omniscience, and infinite being.

The six ancillary scriptures to the *Devimahatmya* are also called limbs. These are the prayers to be offered before and after chanting the main scripture.

In a literal sense, we might also note that both Siva and the Goddess are often depicted with four arms and two legs, or six limbs.

[31] The six qualities of inner fulfillment may be beauty, virtue, influence, abundance, wisdom, and compassion.

[32] *Nirvana* refers to awakened consciousness or liberation. It literally means extinguished, or without air.

When the soul merges with its source, we live without the breath of life, just as the fetus lives in the womb of the mother. The example of a fetus in the womb does not imply regression. It simply illustrates that we can live without breath, as in the state of meditative union, perhaps with the Divine Mother.

Through meditation, the individual is absorbed by its source. Just as the waters of a stream are no longer distinguishable once they have flowed into the ocean, so the individual mind becomes one with all consciousness. *Nirvana* is akin to the Hindu experience of *samadhi*.

[33] Just as twilight is the transitional hour between day and night, so the Goddess is the bridge between this world and transcendence.

[34] *Kundalini*.

[35] The third eye, or the *ajna cakra*, is the seat of intuition.

[36] The sixth sense is that of mind. The five senses (sight, sound, taste, touch, and smell) have to do with the physical world. Through

the sixth sense, subtle reality is experienced. Thought. Dream. Intuition.

[37] All directions include those marked by the compass, those beyond, and those within.

[38] *Svaha* is the *mantra* uttered when oblations are offered into the sacred fire. To make an offering of rice or *ghee* into the fire symbolizes not only generosity, sacrifice, and worship, but also transformation. The fire ceremony is said to clear our mental impurities, as well as difficulties that we are facing in our lives.

Svaha is to say, I surrender all to you, Lord.

Svaha is also a name for the wife of Agni, the Hindu god of fire. Perhaps Agni is the light of a fire and Svaha is the heat, or the other way around. In any case, they are inseparable. When we make offerings into the firepit and call out *svaha*, we are opening to Divine union.

[39] *Svadha* is the oblation offered into a ceremonial fire. The greatest offering, of course, is to offer our innermost essence to the world, and to God.

[40] The four ages, or *yugas*, are said to be gold, silver, bronze, and iron. The ages cycle. As we move through the Iron Age, so we come full circle back to the Golden Age.

It is said that the greatest spiritual practice we can perform during this Iron Age, or Kali Yuga, in which selfishness far outweighs the *dharma*, is the chanting of the divine name. The *Sri Lalita Sahasranama* is one such chanting practice. Another is to sing *bhajans*, devotional hymns, or *kirtan*, simple *mantra* set to music. Chanting can be thought of as meditating aloud. The mind is focused on *mantra*, just as it might be in silent meditation.

[41] The *srividya mantra* is *ka e i la hrim ha sa ka ha la hrim sa ka la hrim.* In Sanskrit, "e" is pronounced "ay," while "i" is pronounced "ee."

This *mantra* is said to represent the causal, subtle, and physical form of the Goddess. Her causal body is *ka e i la hrim*. Her subtle body is said to be *ha sa ka ha la hrim*. Her physical body is represented by the syllables *sa ka la hrim*. The causal body is that from which the subtle and physical bodies are born. The subtle body is that of mind and intellect. The physical body is that of form and sense experience.

42 The sixteenth syllable is said to be a secret that can be revealed only by the *guru*.

43 The three worlds, or planes of existence, are the solid earth, the subtle heavens, and the causal realm, from which earth and heavens are born. Together, the three planes of experience are referred to as *triloka*. They are saluted in the first line of the Gayatri *mantra* as *bhuh*, *bhuvah*, and *svah*. The full *mantra* is chanted for liberation as *om bhur bhuvah svah, tat savitur varenyam, bhargo devasya dhimahi, dhiyo yo nah pracodayat*. It means, "We salute the earth, the heavens, and beyond. We meditate on the light of consciousness, self-illuminating like the sun. Just as the sun lights this world, may the light of awakened consciousness illuminate all."

44 Yak-tail fans.

45 Sets of three are popular in Hindu lore. A trinity may refer to time, in terms of past, present, and future. It may refer to the material, subtle, and causal worlds, from which all experience emanates. It may be the cycle of creation: birth, maturation, and death. It is Brahma, the creator, Visnu, who supports creation, and Siva, who brings about transformation.

The trinity also refers to the three streams of life energy: the *ida*, *pingala*, and *susumna nadis*. *Ida* is cooling and calming moon energy. *Pingala* is the active and fiery sun energy. These energies are similar to *yin* and *yang* in Chinese philosophy. They are interconnected. One gives rise to the other. Together, they become the whole.

These two *nadis* flow up from the base of the spine, *ida* from the left, and *pingala* from the right. They spiral upwards. They cross each other at seven energy vortices called *cakras*. When *ida* and *pingala* are balanced, they merge in the central *susumna nadi*. As energy rises through the *susumna nadi* to the crown of the head, the *yogi* realizes the bliss of spiritual union.

[46] According to Patanjali's *Yoga Sutras*, the eight limbs of yoga are self-control, kind action, easeful posture, mastery of life force, retreat from sense experience, concentration, meditation, and absorption. They are known as *yama*, *niyama*, *asana*, *pranayama*, *pratyahara*, *dharana*, *dhyana*, and *samadhi*.

This path is known as *Raja* or *Ashtanga Yoga*. These eight limbs of *yoga* are often imagined as a ladder, with each rung leading to the next one up.

The eight limbs may also be understood as the spokes of a wheel. Any limb or spoke, when practiced with diligence and sincerity, leads to the center.

Certainly, all of the limbs are beneficial and complementary to each other.

[47] A reference to Sri Krisna.

[48] *Prarabdha karma* is present experience that is the result of our past actions. Those seeds planted which have begun to fructify.

Depending upon the intention behind our actions in the present, we may experience pleasant or painful results in the future. *Sanchita karma* is the storehouse of seeds from past action that have yet to sprout. *Agami karma* (future experience) is determined by how we react to our present situation. Our response to present circumstances plants seeds for *agami karma*. These seeds are stored as *sanchita karma* and then bear fruit as *prarabdha karma*.

Karmic repercussion can most easily be alleviated by being kind in the present. *Yoga Sutra* II.16 states, *Heyam dukham anagatam*. Future suffering can be avoided.

It is important not to compound our present suffering by causing further harm in the current situation. Reacting with aggression only perpetuates the *karmic* cycle. It keeps the pendulum swinging back and forth between action and reaction. Rather than reacting, we can simply experience. Better yet, we can respond with kindness.

It is said that all circumstance is an expression of Divine love, a call to return to the heart. Through sincere effort to make reparation for past action and to change hurtful behaviors in the present, as well as through grace, our past debts are forgiven.

[49] The Four Noble Truths as put forth by Siddhartha Gautama Buddha may be understood as follows: The unenlightened suffer. Suffering arises when we mistake ephemeral experience for truth. When we stop grasping at illusion, we can be free from suffering. To be free, we realize truth. (We can realize truth by following the Eightfold Path: right view, right intention, right speech, right action, right livelihood, right mindfulness, right effort, and right meditation.)

[49] Because the Goddess lives in union with eternal truth, She sports and plays in the ever-changing world. She knows no suffering, for she is not attached to ephemeral objects or situations.

[50] According to Vedic lore, the swan is a sacred symbol of discrimination. The swan summers on the sacred Lake Manasarovar, eats pearls, and can separate milk from water, when the two are mixed.

As the swan separates milk from water, so can we distinguish between what is useful and what is not, though they may be intermingled.

The wise seek lasting bliss rather than the fleeting sensory pleasures of the world.

[51] The Sanskrit alphabet is often referred to as *varnamala*, a wreath of letters. The sounds are said to be *aksara samamnaya*, or indestructible wisdom.

[52] The wheel of illusion, or *samsara*, is a metaphor for the endless cycle of unfulfilled desire. Sometimes, we can't get what we think we need. Another scenario is this: We attain a desired object and then worry over maintaining it. If the pleasure is superficial, we tire of it and turn our attention to a new object of desire. The point is that no sense object can bring lasting inner fulfillment. If we base happiness on an external object or condition, we will always feel that we are missing something.

Think of trying to satisfy hunger simply by looking at a sumptuous meal. A deep hunger cannot be satisfied by the sense of sight. In fact, looking at food without eating may only increase our hunger.

Just so, spiritual longing cannot be fulfilled by gratifying the body or mind.

Sensory pleasure points to spiritual fulfillment. Sensory pleasure is a passing and momentary reminder of the bliss within. We often think that we need something of the world to gratify the senses, including the mind, when really we feel spiritual longing.

Once we get a taste of inner bliss, we turn our attention wholeheartedly inward for true fulfillment that does not depend on ephemeral circumstance, or on gratification of body or mind.

[53] We are said to be reborn upon vowing to live as a renunciate.

[54] A *mahavakya* is a great saying.

"Thou art That," or in Sanskrit, *Tat tvam asi*, equates the soul with transcendent consciousness. It is revealed through the *Candogya Upanisad.*

"That," or true being, is said to be both immanent and transcendent. It is within each of us and beyond all.

According to ancient lore, the Lord became momentarily overwhelmed by people's innumerable requests of him. They prayed for everything from wealth to power to beauty and beyond.

"Why don't people just ask for enlightenment?" He wondered. "Then they would be completely and eternally satisfied."

Still, the unending requests poured in.

The Lord decided to hide. After considering several little-known and distant places, He suddenly realized where most people would never think to look: within their own hearts.

So it is said that the Lord dwells in the cave of the heart. Intimately close, and yet so often overlooked as the source of lasting happiness.

At the same time, divine consciousness transcends individual experience.

This apparent paradox may make little sense to the mind. The point is to let go of mind and experience the presence. Ultimately, awareness of body and mind is absorbed into the heart. The space of the heart then merges with all consciousness.

[55] The five rituals of sacrifice include preparation of offerings, purification, the offering of oblations, the chanting of scripture, and meditative absorption.

[56] *Mudra* means cosmic seal.

[57] *Jnana mudra* is to join the thumb to the forefinger as a symbol of cosmic union. It is said to awaken us to the truth within.

PART IV:

Transliteration for Chanting

Dhyānam

sindūrāruṇa-vigrahāṁ tri-nayanām māṇikya mauli-sphurat
tārānāyaka-śekharām smitamukhīm āpīna-vakṣoruhām
pāṇibhyām alipūrṇa-ratna-caṣakam raktotpalam bibhratīm
saumyāṁ ratna-ghaṭastha-rakta caraṇāṁ dhyāyetparāmambikām

dhyāyet padmāsanasthām vikasita-vadanām
padma-patrāyatākṣīm
hemābhām pītavastrām kara-kalita-lasad
hema padmām varāṅgīm
sarvālaṅkāra-yuktām satatam-abhayadām
bhakta-namrām bhavānīm
śrīvīdyām śāntamūrtim sakala-sura-nutāṁ
sarva sampat pradātrīm

sakuṅkuma-vilepanām alika-cumbi-kastūrikām
samanda-hasitekṣaṇām saśara-cāpa-pāśāṅkuśām
aśeṣa-jana-mohinīm aruṇa-mālya-bhūṣojvalām
japā-kusuma-bhāsurām japavidhau smaredambikām

aruṇāṁ karuṇā-taraṅgitākṣīṁ
dhṛta-pāśāṅkuśa-puṣpa-bāṇa-cāpām
aṇimādibhir āvṛtām mayūkhai
raham-ityeva vibhāvaye māheśīm

Śrī Lalitā Sahasranāmāvaliḥ

Oṁ śrī-mātre namaḥ
Oṁ śrī-mahā-rājñyai namaḥ
Oṁ śrīmat-simhāsan’eśvaryai namaḥ
Oṁ cid-agni-kuṇḍa-sambhūtāyai namaḥ
Oṁ deva-kārya-samudyatāyai namaḥ
Oṁ udyad-bhānu-sahasrābhāyai namaḥ
Oṁ catur-bāhu-samanvitāyai namaḥ
Oṁ rāga-svarūpa-pāśāḍhyāyai namaḥ
Oṁ krodhā-kār’āṅkuś’ojjvalāyai namaḥ
Oṁ mano-rūp’ekṣu-kodaṇḍāyai namaḥ 10
Oṁ pañca-tanmātra-sāyakāyai namaḥ
Oṁ nij’āruṇa-prabhā-pūra-majjad-brahmāṇḍa-maṇḍalāyai namaḥ
Oṁ campak’āśoka-punnāga-saugandhika-lasat-kacāyai namaḥ
Oṁ kuruvinda-maṇi-śreṇī-kanat-koṭīra-maṇḍitāyai namaḥ
Oṁ aṣṭamī-candra-vibrājadalika-sthala-śobhitāyai namaḥ
Oṁ mukha-candra-kalaṅkābha mṛganābhi-viśeṣakāyai namaḥ
Oṁ vadana-smara-māṅgalya-gṛha-toraṇa-cillikāyai namaḥ
Oṁ vaktra-lakṣmī-parīvāha-calan-mīnābha-locanāyai namaḥ
Oṁ nava-campaka-puṣpābha-nāsā-daṇḍa-virā-jitāyai namaḥ
Oṁ tārā-kānti-tiraskāri-nāsābharaṇa-bhāsurāyai
namaḥ 20
Oṁ kadamba-mañjarī-kḷpta-karṇapūra-manoharāyai namaḥ
Oṁ tāṭaṅka-yugalī-bhūta-tapan’oḍupa-maṇḍalāyai namaḥ
Oṁ padma-rāga śil’ādarśa-paribhāvi-kapola-bhuve namaḥ
Oṁ nava-vidruma-bimba-śrī-nyakkāri-radana-cchadāyai namaḥ
Oṁ śuddha vidyā’ṅkurākāra-dvija-paṅkti-dvay’ojjvalāyai namaḥ
Oṁ karpūra-vīṭik’āmoda-samākarṣi-digantarāyai namaḥ
Oṁ nija-sallāpa-mādhurya-vinirbhartsita-kacchapyai namaḥ
Oṁ manda-smita-prabhā-pūra-majjat-kāmeśa-mānasāyai namaḥ
Oṁ anākalita-sādṛśya-cibuka-śrī-virājitāyai namaḥ

Oṁ kām'eśa-baddha-māṅgalya-sūtra-śobhita-kandharāyai namaḥ 30
Oṁ kanak'āṅgada-keyūra-kamanīya-bhuj'ān-vitāyai namaḥ
Oṁ ratna-graiveya-cintāka-lola-muktāphal'ān-vitāyai namaḥ
Oṁ kām'eśvara-prema-ratna-maṇi-pratipaṇa-stanyai namaḥ
Oṁ nābhy'ālavāla-romāli-latā-phala-kuca-dvayyai namaḥ
Oṁ lakṣya-roma-latā-dhāratā-samunneya-madhyamāyai namaḥ
Oṁ stana-bhāra dalan-madhya-paṭṭa-bandha-vali-trayāyai namaḥ
Oṁ aruṇ'āruṇa-kausumbha-vastra-bhāsvat-kaṭī-taṭyai namaḥ
Oṁ ratna-kiṅkiṇik'āramya-raśanā-dāma-bhūṣitāyai namaḥ
Oṁ kāmeśa-jñāta-saubhāgya-mārdav'oru-dvay'ānvitāyai namaḥ
Oṁ māṇikya-mukuṭ'ākāra jānu-dvaya-virājitāyai namaḥ 40
Oṁ indra-gopa-parikṣipta-smara-tūṇābha-jaṅghikāyai namaḥ
Oṁ gūḍha-gulphāyai namaḥ
Oṁ kūrma-pṛṣṭha-jayiṣṇu-prapad'ānvitāyai namaḥ
Oṁ nakha-dīdhiti-saṁchanna-namajjana-tamo-guṇāyai namaḥ
Oṁ pada-dvaya-prabhā-jāla-parākṛta-saroruhāyai namaḥ
Oṁ siñjāna-maṇi-mañjīra-maṇḍita-śrīpad'āmbujāyai namaḥ
Oṁ marālī-manda-gamanāyai namaḥ
Oṁ mahā-lāvaṇya-śevadhaye namaḥ
Oṁ sarv'āruṇāyai namaḥ
Oṁ anavadyā'ṅgyai namaḥ 50
Oṁ sarv'ābharaṇa-bhūṣitāyai namaḥ
Oṁ śiva-kāmeśvar'āṅkasthāyai namaḥ
Oṁ śivāyai namaḥ
Oṁ svādhīna-vallabhāyai namaḥ
Oṁ sumeru-madhya-śṛṅga-sthāyai namaḥ
Oṁ śrīman-nagara-nāyikāyai namaḥ
Oṁ cintāmaṇi-gṛh'āntasthāyai namaḥ
Oṁ pañca-brahm'āsana-sthitāyai namaḥ
Oṁ mahā-padm'āṭavī-samsthāyai namaḥ
Oṁ kadamba-vana-vāsinyai namaḥ 60
Oṁ sudhā-sāgara-madhyasthāyai namaḥ
Oṁ kāmākṣyai namah

Oṁ kāma-dāyinyai namaḥ
Oṁ devarṣi-gaṇa-saṅghāta-stūyamān'ātma-vaibhavāyai namaḥ
Oṁ bhaṇḍ'āsura-vadho'dyukta-śakti-senā-saman-vitāyai namaḥ
Oṁ sampatkarī-samārūḍha-sindhura-vraja-sevitāyai namaḥ
Oṁ aśvārūḍh'ādhiṣṭhit'āśva-koṭi-koṭibhir-āvṛtāyai namaḥ
Oṁ cakra-rāja-rath'ārūḍha sarv'āyudha pariṣkṛtāyai namaḥ
Oṁ geya-cakra-rath'ārūḍha-mantriṇī pari-sevitāyai namaḥ
Oṁ kiri-cakra rath'ārūḍha-daṇḍa-nāthā puras-kṛtāyai namaḥ 70
Oṁ jvālā-mālinik'ākṣipta-vahni-prākāra-madhya-gāyai namaḥ
Oṁ bhaṇḍa-sainya-vadh'odyukta-śakti-vikrama-harṣitāyai namaḥ
Oṁ nityā-parākram'āṭopa-nirkṣaṇa-samutsukāyai namaḥ
Oṁ bhaṇḍa-putra-vadh'odyukta-bālā-vikrama-nanditāyai namaḥ
Oṁ mantriṇy'ambā-viracita-viṣaṅga-vadha-toṣitāyai namaḥ
Oṁ viśukra-prāṇa-haraṇa-vārāhī-vīrya-nanditāyai namaḥ
Oṁ kāmeśvara-mukh'āloka-kalpita-śrī-gaṇeśvarāyai namaḥ
Oṁ mahā-gaṇeśa-nirbhinna-vighna-yantra-prahar-ṣitāyai namaḥ
Oṁ bhaṇḍāsur'endra-nirmukta-śastra-pratyastra-varṣiṇyai namaḥ
Oṁ karāṅguli-nakh'otpanna-nārāyaṇa-daśākṛtyai namaḥ 80
Oṁ mahā-pāśupat'āstr'āgni-nirdagdh'āsura-sainikāyai namaḥ
Oṁ kāmeśvar'āstra-nirdagdha-sabhaṇḍ'āsura śūnyakāyai namaḥ
Oṁ brahm'opendra-mahendrādi-deva-saṁstuta-vaibhavāyai namaḥ
Oṁ hara-netr'āgni-sandagdha-kāma-sañjīvan'auṣadhyai namaḥ
Oṁ śrīmad-vāgbhava-kūṭ'aika-svarūpa-mukha-paṅkajāyai namaḥ
Oṁ kaṇṭhādhaḥ-kaṭi-paryanta-madhya-kūṭa-svarūpiṇyai namaḥ
Oṁ śakti-kūṭ'aikaṭāpanna-kaṭyadho-bhāga-dhāriṇyai namaḥ
Oṁ mūla-mantr'ātmikāyai namaḥ
Oṁ mūla-kūṭa-traya-kalebarāyai namaḥ
Oṁ kul'āmṛt'aika-rasikāyai namaḥ 90
Oṁ kula-saṅketa-pālinyai namaḥ
Oṁ kul'āṅganāyai namaḥ
Oṁ kul'āntasthāyai namaḥ
Oṁ kaulinyai namaḥ

Oṁ kula-yoginyai namaḥ
Oṁ akulāyai namaḥ
Oṁ samay'āntasthāyai namaḥ
Oṁ samay'ācāra-tatparāyai namaḥ
Oṁ mūl'ādhār'aika-nilayāyai namaḥ
Oṁ brahma-granthi-vibhedinyai namaḥ 100
Oṁ maṇipūr'āntar-uditāyai namaḥ
Oṁ viṣṇu-granthi-vibhedinyai namaḥ
Oṁ ājñā-cakr'āntarālasthāyai namaḥ
Oṁ rudra-granthi-vibhedinyai namaḥ
Oṁ sahasrār'āmbuj'ārūḍhāyai namaḥ
Oṁ sudhā-sār'ābhivarṣiṇyai namaḥ
Oṁ taḍil-latā-sama-rucyai namaḥ
Oṁ ṣaṭ-cakr'opari-samsthitāyai namaḥ
Oṁ mah'āsaktyai namaḥ
Oṁ kuṇḍalinyai namaḥ 110
Oṁ bisa-tantu-tanīyasyai namaḥ
Oṁ bhavānyai namaḥ
Oṁ bhāvanā-gamyāyai namaḥ
Oṁ bhav'āraṇya-kuṭhārikāyai namaḥ
Oṁ bhadra-priyāyai namaḥ
Oṁ bhadra-mūrtaye namaḥ
Oṁ bhakta-saubhāgya-dāyinyai namaḥ
Oṁ bhakti-priyāyai namaḥ
Oṁ bhakti-gamyāyai namaḥ
Oṁ bhakti-vaśyāyai namaḥ 120
Oṁ bhay'āpahāyai namaḥ
Oṁ śāmbhavyai namaḥ
Oṁ śārad'ārādhyāyai namaḥ
Oṁ śarvāṇyai namaḥ
Oṁ śarma-dāyinyai namaḥ
Oṁ śāṅkaryai namaḥ
Oṁ śrīkaryai namaḥ
Oṁ sādhvyai namaḥ
Oṁ śarac-candra-nibh'ānanā'yai namaḥ

Oṁ śāt'odaryai namaḥ 130
Oṁ śāntimatyai namaḥ
Oṁ nirādhārāyai namaḥ
Oṁ nirañjanāyai namaḥ
Oṁ nirlepāyai namaḥ
Oṁ nirmalāyai namaḥ
Oṁ nityāyai namaḥ
Oṁ nirākārāyai namaḥ
Oṁ nirākulāyai namaḥ
Oṁ nirguṇāyai namaḥ
Oṁ niṣkalāyai namaḥ 140
Oṁ śāntāyai namaḥ
Oṁ niṣkāmāyai namaḥ
Oṁ nir-upaplavāyai namaḥ
Oṁ nitya-muktāyai namaḥ
Oṁ nirvikārāyai namaḥ
Oṁ niṣprapañcāyai namaḥ
Oṁ nirāśrayāyai namaḥ
Oṁ nitya-śuddhāyai namaḥ
Oṁ nitya-buddhāyai namaḥ
Oṁ nir-avadyāyai namaḥ 150
Oṁ nir-antarāyai namaḥ
Oṁ niṣ-kāraṇāyai namaḥ
Oṁ niṣ-kalaṅkāyai namaḥ
Oṁ nir-upādhaye namaḥ
Oṁ nir-īśvarāyai namaḥ
Oṁ nirāgāyai namaḥ
Oṁ rāga-mathanyai namaḥ
Oṁ nir-madāyai namaḥ
Oṁ mada-nāśinyai namaḥ
Oṁ niścintāyai namaḥ 160
Oṁ nir-ahaṅkārāyai namaḥ
Oṁ nir-mohāyai namaḥ
Oṁ moha-nāśinyai namaḥ
Oṁ nir-mamāyai namaḥ

Oṁ mamatā-hantryai namaḥ
Oṁ niṣpāpāyai namaḥ
Oṁ pāpa-nāśinyai namaḥ
Oṁ niṣkrodhāyai namaḥ
Oṁ krodha-śamanyai namaḥ
Oṁ nir-lobhāyai namaḥ 170
Oṁ lobha-nāśinyai namaḥ
Oṁ niḥsaṁśayāyai namaḥ
Oṁ saṁśayaghnyai namaḥ
Oṁ nir-bhavāyai namaḥ
Oṁ bhava-nāśinyai namaḥ
Oṁ nir-vikalpāyai namaḥ
Oṁ nir'ābādhāyai namaḥ
Oṁ nir-bhedāyai namaḥ
Oṁ bheda-nāśinyai namaḥ
Oṁ nirnāśāyai namaḥ 180
Oṁ mṛtyu-mathanyai namaḥ
Oṁ niṣkriyāyai namaḥ
Oṁ niṣparigrahāyai namaḥ
Oṁ nistulāyai namaḥ
Oṁ nīla-cikurāyai namaḥ
Oṁ nir-apāyāyai namaḥ
Oṁ niratyayāyai namaḥ
Oṁ durlabhāyai namaḥ
Oṁ durgamāyai namaḥ
Oṁ durgāyai namaḥ 190
Oṁ duḥkha-hantryai namaḥ
Oṁ sukha-pradāyai namaḥ
Oṁ duṣṭa-dūrāyai namaḥ
Oṁ dur'ācāra śamanyai namaḥ
Oṁ doṣa-varjitāyai namaḥ
Oṁ sarva-jñāyai namaḥ
Oṁ sāndra-karuṇāyai namaḥ
Oṁ samān'ādhika varjitāyai namaḥ
Oṁ sarva-śakti-mayyai namaḥ

Oṁ sarva-maṅgalāyai namaḥ 200
Oṁ sad-gati-pradāyai namaḥ
Oṁ sarv'eśvaryai namaḥ
Oṁ sarva-mayyai namaḥ
Oṁ sarva-mantra-svarūpiṇyai namaḥ
Oṁ sarva-yantr'ātmikāyai namaḥ
Oṁ sarva-tantra-rūpāyai namaḥ
Oṁ man'onmanyai namaḥ
Oṁ māh'eśvaryai namaḥ
Oṁ mahā-devyai namaḥ
Oṁ mahā-lakṣmyai namaḥ 210
Oṁ mṛḍa-priyāyai namaḥ
Oṁ mahā-rūpāyai namaḥ
Oṁ mahā-pūjyāyai namaḥ
Oṁ mahā-pātaka-nāśinyai namaḥ
Oṁ mahā-māyāyai namaḥ
Oṁ mahā-sattvāyai namaḥ
Oṁ mahā-śaktyai namaḥ
Oṁ mahā-ratyai namaḥ
Oṁ mahā-bhogāyai namaḥ
Oṁ mah'aiśvaryāyai namaḥ 220
Oṁ mahā-vīryāyai namaḥ
Oṁ mahā-balāyai namaḥ
Oṁ mahā-buddhyai namaḥ
Oṁ mahā-siddhyai namaḥ
Oṁ mahā-yog'eśvar'eśvaryai namaḥ
Oṁ mahā-tantrāyai namaḥ
Oṁ mahā-mantrāyai namaḥ
Oṁ mahā-yantrāyai namaḥ
Oṁ mah'āsanāyai namaḥ
Oṁ mahā-yāga-kram'ārādhyāyai namaḥ 230
Oṁ mahā-bhairava-pūjitāyai namaḥ
Oṁ mah'eśvara-mahā-kalpa-mahā'taṇḍava-sākṣiṇyai namaḥ
Oṁ mahā-kāmeśa-mahiṣyai namaḥ
Oṁ mahā-tripura-sundaryai namaḥ

Oṁ catuḥ-ṣaṣṭ'yupacār'āḍhyāyai namaḥ
Oṁ catuḥ-ṣaṣṭi-kalā-mayyai namaḥ
Oṁ mahā-catuḥ-ṣaṣṭi-koṭi-yoginī-gaṇa-sevitāyai namaḥ
Oṁ manu-vidyāyai namaḥ
Oṁ candra-vidyāyai namaḥ
Oṁ candra-maṇḍala-madhyagāyai namaḥ 240
Oṁ cāru-rūpāyai namaḥ
Oṁ cāru-hāsāyai namaḥ
Oṁ cāru-candra-kalā-dharāyai namaḥ
Oṁ car'ācara-jagan-nāthāyai namaḥ
Oṁ cakra-rāja-niketanāyai namaḥ
Oṁ pārvatyai namaḥ
Oṁ padma-nayanāyai namaḥ
Oṁ padma-rāga-sama-prabhāyai namaḥ
Oṁ pañca-pretāsan'āsīnāyai namaḥ
Oṁ pañca-brahma-svarūpiṇyai namaḥ 250
Oṁ cinmayyai namaḥ
Oṁ param'ānandāyai namaḥ
Oṁ vijñāna-ghana-rūpiṇyai namaḥ
Oṁ dhyāna-dhyātṛ-dhyeya-rūpāyai namaḥ
Oṁ dharm'ādharma-vivarjitāyai namaḥ
Oṁ viśva-rūpāyai namaḥ
Oṁ jāgariṇyai namaḥ
Oṁ svapantyai namaḥ
Oṁ taijas'ātmikāyai namaḥ
Oṁ suptāyai namaḥ 260
Oṁ prājñ'ātmikāyai namaḥ
Oṁ turyāyai namaḥ
Oṁ sarv'āvasthā-vivarjitāyai namaḥ
Oṁ sṛṣṭi-kartryai namaḥ
Oṁ brahma-rūpāyai namaḥ
Oṁ goptryai namaḥ
Oṁ govinda-rūpiṇyai namaḥ
Oṁ samhāriṇyai namaḥ
Oṁ rudra-rūpāyai namaḥ

Oṁ tirodhāna-karyai namaḥ 270
Oṁ īśvaryai namaḥ
Oṁ sadā-śivāyai namaḥ
Oṁ anugraha-dāyai namaḥ
Oṁ pañca-kṛtya-parāyaṇāyai namaḥ
Oṁ bhānu-maṇḍala-madhyasthāyai namaḥ
Oṁ bhairavyai namaḥ
Oṁ bhaga-mālinyai namaḥ
Oṁ pad'māsanāyai namaḥ
Oṁ bhagavatyai namaḥ
Oṁ padma-nābha-sahodaryai namaḥ 280
Oṁ unmeṣa-nimiṣ'otpanna-vipanna-bhuvan'āvalyai namaḥ
Oṁ sahasra-śīṛsa-vadanāyai namaḥ
Oṁ sahasr'ākṣyai namaḥ
Oṁ sahasra-pade namaḥ
Oṁ ābrahma-kīṭa-jananyai namaḥ
Oṁ varṇ'āśrama-vidhāyinyai namaḥ
Oṁ nij'ājñā-rūpa-nigamāyai namaḥ
Oṁ puṇy'āpuṇya-phala-pradāyai namaḥ
Oṁ śruti-sīmanta-sindūrī-kṛta-pād'ābja-dhūlikāyai namaḥ
Oṁ sakal'āgama-sandoha-śukti-sampuṭa-mauktikāyai
namaḥ 290
Oṁ puruṣ'ārtha-pradāyai namaḥ
Oṁ pūrṇāyai namaḥ
Oṁ bhoginyai namaḥ
Oṁ bhuvan'eśvaryai namaḥ
Oṁ ambikāyai namaḥ
Oṁ anādi-nidhanāyai namaḥ
Oṁ hari-brahm'endra-sevitāyai namaḥ
Oṁ nārāyaṇyai namaḥ
Oṁ nāda-rūpāyai namaḥ
Oṁ nāma-rūpa-vivarjitāyai namaḥ 300
Oṁ hrīṅ-kāryai namaḥ
Oṁ hrīmatyai namaḥ
Oṁ hṛdyāyai namaḥ

Oṁ hey'opādeya-varjitāyai namaḥ
Oṁ rāja-rāj'ārcitāyai namaḥ
Oṁ rājñyai namaḥ
Oṁ ramyāyai namaḥ
Oṁ rājīva-locanāyai namaḥ
Oṁ rañjanyai namaḥ
Oṁ ramaṇyai namaḥ 310
Oṁ rasyāyai namaḥ
Oṁ raṇat-kiṅkiṇi-mekhalāyai namaḥ
Oṁ ramāyai namaḥ
Oṁ rākendu-vadanāyai namaḥ
Oṁ rati-rūpāyai namaḥ
Oṁ rati-priyāyai namaḥ
Oṁ rakṣā-karyai namaḥ
Oṁ rākṣasa-ghnyai namaḥ
Oṁ rāmāyai namaḥ
Oṁ ramaṇa-lampaṭāyai namaḥ 320
Oṁ kāmyāyai namaḥ
Oṁ kāma-kalā-rūpāyai namaḥ
Oṁ kadamba-kusuma-priyāyai namaḥ
Oṁ kalyāṇyai namaḥ
Oṁ jagatī-kandāyai namaḥ
Oṁ karuṇā-rasa-sāgarāyai namaḥ
Oṁ kalāvatyai namaḥ
Oṁ kal'ālāpāyai namaḥ
Oṁ kāntāyai namaḥ
Oṁ kādambarī-priyāyai namaḥ 330
Oṁ varadāyai namaḥ
Oṁ vāma-nayanāyai namaḥ
Oṁ vāruṇī-mada-vihvalāyai namaḥ
Oṁ viśv'ādhikāyai namaḥ
Oṁ veda-vedyāyai namaḥ
Oṁ vindhy'ācala-nivāsinyai namaḥ
Oṁ vidhātryai namaḥ
Oṁ veda-jananyai namaḥ

Oṁ viṣṇu-māyāyai namaḥ
Oṁ vilāsinyai namaḥ 340
Oṁ kṣetra-svarūpāyai namaḥ
Oṁ kṣetr'eśyai namaḥ
Oṁ kṣetra-kṣetrajña pālinyai namaḥ
Oṁ kṣaya-vṛddhi-vinirmuktāyai namaḥ
Oṁ kṣetra-pāla-samarcitāyai namaḥ
Oṁ vijayāyai namaḥ
Oṁ vimalāyai namaḥ
Oṁ vandyāyai namaḥ
Oṁ vandāru-jana-vatsalāyai namaḥ
Oṁ vāg-vādinyai namaḥ 350
Oṁ vāma-keśyai namaḥ
Oṁ vahni-maṇḍala-vāsinyai namaḥ
Oṁ bhaktimat-kalpa-latikāyai namaḥ
Oṁ paśu-pāśa-vimocinyai namaḥ
Oṁ samhṛtāśeṣa-pāṣaṇḍāyai namaḥ
Oṁ sadācāra-pravartikāyai namaḥ
Oṁ tāpa-tray'āgni-santapta-sam'āhlādana-candrikāyai namaḥ
Oṁ taruṇyai namaḥ
Oṁ tāpas'ārādhyāyai namaḥ
Oṁ tanu-madhyāyai namaḥ 360
Oṁ tam'opahāyai namaḥ
Oṁ cityai namaḥ
Oṁ tat-pada lakṣ'yārthāyai namaḥ
Oṁ cid-eka-rasa-rūpiṇyai namaḥ
Oṁ sv'ātm'ānandalavī-bhūta-brahmādyānanda-santatyai namaḥ
Oṁ parāyai namaḥ
Oṁ pratyak-citī-rūpāyai namaḥ
Oṁ paśyantyai namaḥ
Oṁ para-devatāyai namaḥ
Oṁ madhyamāyai namaḥ 370
Oṁ vaikharī-rūpāyai namaḥ
Oṁ bhakta-mānasa-hamsikāyai namaḥ
Oṁ kāmeśvara-prāṇa-nāḍyai namaḥ

Oṁ kṛtajñāyai namaḥ
Oṁ kāma-pūjitāyai namaḥ
Oṁ śṛṅgāra-rasa-sampūrṇāyai namaḥ
Oṁ jayāyai namaḥ
Oṁ jālandhara-sthitāyai namaḥ
Oṁ oḍyāṇa-pīṭha-nilayāyai namaḥ
Oṁ bindu-maṇḍala-vāsinyai namaḥ 380
Oṁ raho-yāga-kram'ārādhyāyai namaḥ
Oṁ rahas-tarpaṇa-tarpitāyai namaḥ
Oṁ sadyaḥ-prasādinyai namaḥ
Oṁ viśva-sākṣiṇyai namaḥ
Oṁ sākṣi-varjitāyai namaḥ
Oṁ ṣaḍaṅga-devatā-yuktāyai namaḥ
Oṁ ṣāḍguṇya-pari-pūritāyai namaḥ
Oṁ nitya-klinnāyai namaḥ
Oṁ nirupamāyai namaḥ
Oṁ nirvāṇa-sukha-dāyinyai namaḥ 390
Oṁ nityā-ṣoḍaśikā-rūpāyai namaḥ
Oṁ śrīkaṇṭhārdha-śarīriṇyai namaḥ
Oṁ prabhāvatyai namaḥ
Oṁ prabhā-rūpāyai namaḥ
Oṁ prasiddhāyai namaḥ
Oṁ param'eśvaryai namaḥ
Oṁ mūla-prakṛtyai namaḥ
Oṁ avyaktāyai namaḥ
Oṁ vyakt'āvyakta-svarūpiṇyai namaḥ
Oṁ vyāpinyai namaḥ 400
Oṁ vividh'ākārāyai namaḥ
Oṁ vidy'āvidyā-svarūpiṇyai namaḥ
Oṁ mahā-kāmeśa-nayana-kumud'āhlāda-kaumudyai namaḥ
Oṁ bhakta-hārda-tamo-bheda-bhānumad-bhānu-santatyai namaḥ
Oṁ śiva-dūtyai namaḥ
Oṁ śiv'ārādhyāyai namaḥ
Oṁ śiva-mūrtyai namaḥ
Oṁ śivaṅkaryai namaḥ

Oṁ śiva-priyāyai namaḥ
Oṁ śiva-parāyai namaḥ 410
Oṁ śiṣṭ'eṣṭāyai namaḥ
Oṁ śiṣṭa-pūjitāyai namaḥ
Oṁ aprameyāyai namaḥ
Oṁ svaprakāśāyai namaḥ
Oṁ mano-vācām-agocarāyai namah
Oṁ cicchaktyai namaḥ
Oṁ cetanā-rūpāyai namaḥ
Oṁ jaḍa-śaktyai namaḥ
Oṁ jaḍ'ātmikāyai namaḥ
Oṁ gāyatryai namaḥ 420
Oṁ vyāhṛtyai namaḥ
Oṁ sandhyāyai namaḥ
Oṁ dvija-vṛnda-niṣevitāyai namaḥ
Oṁ tattv'āsanāyai namaḥ
Oṁ tasmai namaḥ
Oṁ tubhyam namaḥ
Oṁ ayyai namaḥ
Oṁ pañca-koś'āntara-sthitāyai namah
Oṁ niḥsma-mahimne namaḥ
Oṁ nitya-yauvanāyai namaḥ 430
Oṁ mada-śālinyai namaḥ
Oṁ mada-ghūrṇita-rakt'ākṣyai namaḥ
Oṁ mada-pāṭala-gaṇḍa-bhuve namaḥ
Oṁ candana-drava-digdhāṅgyai namaḥ
Oṁ cāmpeya-kusuma-priyāyai namaḥ
Oṁ kuśalāyai namaḥ
Oṁ komal'ākārāyai namaḥ
Oṁ kurukullāyai namaḥ
Oṁ kul'eśvaryai namaḥ
Oṁ kula-kuṇḍ'ālayāyai namaḥ 440
Oṁ kaula-mārga-tatpara-sevitāyai namaḥ
Oṁ kumāra-gaṇanāth'āmbāyai namaḥ
Oṁ tuṣṭyai namaḥ

Oṁ puṣṭyai namaḥ
Oṁ matyai namaḥ
Oṁ dhṛtyai namaḥ
Oṁ śāntyai namaḥ
Oṁ svasti-matyai namaḥ
Oṁ kāntyai namaḥ
Oṁ nandinyai namaḥ 450
Oṁ vighna-nāśinyai namaḥ
Oṁ tejovatyai namaḥ
Oṁ tri-nayanāyai namaḥ
Oṁ lolākṣī-kāma-rūpiṇyai namaḥ
Oṁ mālinyai namaḥ
Oṁ haṁsinyai namaḥ
Oṁ mātre namaḥ
Oṁ malay'ācala-vāsinyai namaḥ
Oṁ sumukhyai namaḥ
Oṁ nalinyai namaḥ 460
Oṁ subhruve namaḥ
Oṁ śobhanāyai namaḥ
Oṁ sura-nāyikāyai namaḥ
Oṁ kāla-kaṇṭhyai namaḥ
Oṁ kānti-matyai namaḥ
Oṁ kṣobhiṇyai namaḥ
Oṁ sūkṣma-rūpiṇyai namaḥ
Oṁ vajr'eśvaryai namaḥ
Oṁ vāma-devyai namaḥ
Oṁ vayo'vasthā-vivarjitāyai namaḥ 470
Oṁ siddh'eśvaryai namaḥ
Oṁ siddha-vidyāyai namaḥ
Oṁ siddha-mātre namaḥ
Oṁ yaśasvinyai namaḥ
Oṁ viśuddhi-cakra-nilayāyai namaḥ
Oṁ ārakta-varṇāyai namaḥ
Oṁ tri-locanāyai namaḥ
Oṁ khaṭvāṅgādi-praharaṇāyai namaḥ

Oṁ vadan'aika-samanvitāyai namaḥ

Oṁ pāyas'ānna-priyāyai namaḥ 480

Oṁ tvaksthāyai namaḥ

Oṁ paśu-loka-bhayaṅkaryai namaḥ

Oṁ amṛt'ādi-mahā-śakti-samvṛtāyai namaḥ

Oṁ ḍākin'īśvaryai namaḥ

Oṁ anāhat'ābja-nilayāyai namaḥ

Oṁ śyām'ābhāyai namaḥ

Oṁ vadana-dvayāyai namaḥ

Oṁ damṣṭr'ojjvalāyai namaḥ

Oṁ akṣa-māl'ādi-dharāyai namaḥ

Oṁ rudhira-samsthitāyai namaḥ 490

Oṁ kāla-rātryādi-śakty'aughavṛtāyai namaḥ

Oṁ snigdh'audana priyāyai namaḥ

Oṁ mahā-vīrendra-varadāyai namaḥ

Oṁ rākiṇy'ambā-svarūpiṇyai namaḥ

Oṁ maṇipūr'ābja-nilayāyai namaḥ

Oṁ vadana-traya-samyutāyai namaḥ

Oṁ vajr'ādikāyudhopetāyai namaḥ

Oṁ ḍāmary'ādibhir-āvṛtāyai namaḥ

Oṁ rakta-varṇāyai namaḥ

Oṁ māṁsa-niṣṭhāyai namaḥ 500

Oṁ guḍ'ānna-prīta mānasāyai namaḥ

Oṁ samasta-bhakta-sukhadāyai namaḥ

Oṁ lākiny'ambā-svarūpiṇyai namaḥ

Oṁ svādhiṣṭhān'āmbuja-gatāyai namaḥ

Oṁ catur-vaktra-manoharāyai namaḥ

Oṁ śulādy'āyudha-sampannāyai namaḥ

Oṁ pīta-varṇāyai namaḥ

Oṁ ati-garvitāyai namaḥ

Oṁ medo-niṣṭhāyai namaḥ

Oṁ madhu-prītāyai namaḥ 510

Oṁ bandhiny'ādi-samanvitāyai namaḥ

Oṁ dadhy'annāsakta-hṛdayāyai namaḥ

Oṁ kākinī-rūpa-dhāriṇyai namaḥ

Oṁ mūlādhār'āmbuj'ārūḍhāyai namaḥ
Oṁ pañca-vaktrāyai namaḥ
Oṁ asthi-samsthitāyai namaḥ
Oṁ aṅkuś'ādi-praharaṇāyai namaḥ
Oṁ varad'ādi-niṣevitāyai namaḥ
Oṁ mudg'audan'āsakta-cittāyai namaḥ
Oṁ sākiny'ambā-svarūpiṇyai namaḥ 520
Oṁ ājñā-cakr'ābja-nilayāyai namaḥ
Oṁ śukla-varṇāyai namaḥ
Oṁ ṣaḍ-ānanāyai namaḥ
Oṁ majjā-samsthāyai namaḥ
Oṁ hamsa-vatī-mukhya-śakti-samanvitāyai namaḥ
Oṁ haridr'ānn'aika-rasikāyai namaḥ
Oṁ hākinī-rūpa-dhāriṇyai namaḥ
Oṁ sahasra-dala-padmasthāyai namaḥ
Oṁ sarva-varṇ'opaśobhitāyai namaḥ
Oṁ sarv'āyudha-dharāyai namaḥ 530
Oṁ śukla-samsthitāyai namaḥ
Oṁ sarvato'mukhyai namaḥ
Oṁ sarv'audana-prīta-cittāyai namaḥ
Oṁ yākiny'ambā-svarūpiṇyai namaḥ
Oṁ svāhāyai namaḥ
Oṁ svadhāyai namaḥ
Oṁ amatyai namaḥ
Oṁ medhāyai namaḥ
Oṁ śrutyai namaḥ
Oṁ smṛtyai namaḥ 540
Oṁ anuttamāyai namaḥ
Oṁ puṇya-kīrtyai namaḥ
Oṁ puṇya-labhyāyai namaḥ
Oṁ puṇya-śravaṇa-kīrtanāyai namaḥ
Oṁ pulomaj'ārcitāyai namaḥ
Oṁ bandha-mocanyai namaḥ
Oṁ barbar'ālakāyai namaḥ
Oṁ vimarśa-rūpiṇyai namaḥ

Oṁ vidyāyai namaḥ
Oṁ viyad'ādi-jagat-prasuve namaḥ 550
Oṁ sarva-vyādhi-praśamanyai namaḥ
Oṁ sarva-mṛtyu-nivāriṇyai namaḥ
Oṁ agra-gaṇyāyai namaḥ
Oṁ acintya-rūpāyai namaḥ
Oṁ kali-kalmaṣa-nāśinyai namaḥ
Oṁ kātyāyanyai namaḥ
Oṁ kāla-hantryai namaḥ
Oṁ kamalākṣa-niṣevitāyai namaḥ
Oṁ tāmbūla-pūrita-mukhyai namaḥ
Oṁ dāḍimī-kusuma-prabhāyai namaḥ 560
Oṁ mṛgākṣyai namaḥ
Oṁ mohinyai namaḥ
Oṁ mukhyāyai namaḥ
Oṁ mṛḍānyai namaḥ
Oṁ mitra-rūpiṇyai namaḥ
Oṁ nitya-tṛptāyai namaḥ
Oṁ bhakta-nidhaye namaḥ
Oṁ niyantryai namaḥ
Oṁ nikhil'eśvaryai namaḥ
Oṁ maitry'ādi-vāsanā-labhyāyai namaḥ 570
Oṁ mahā-pralaya-sākṣiṇyai namaḥ
Oṁ parāśaktyai namaḥ
Oṁ parāniṣṭhāyai namaḥ
Oṁ prajñāna-ghana-rūpiṇyai namaḥ
Oṁ mādhvī-pān'ālasāyai namaḥ
Oṁ mattāyai namaḥ
Oṁ mātṛkā-varṇa-rūpiṇyai namaḥ
Oṁ mahā-kailāsa-nilayāyai namaḥ
Oṁ mṛṇāla-mṛdu-dor-latāyai namaḥ
Oṁ mahanīyāyai namaḥ 580
Oṁ dayā-mūrtyai namaḥ
Oṁ mahā-sāṁrājya-śālinyai namaḥ
Oṁ ātma-vidyāyai namaḥ

Oṁ mahā-vidyāyai namaḥ
Oṁ śrī-vidyāyai namaḥ
Oṁ kāma-sevitāyai namaḥ
Oṁ śrī-ṣoḍaśākṣarī-vidyāyai namaḥ
Oṁ trikūṭāyai namaḥ
Oṁ kāma-koṭikāyai namaḥ
Oṁ kaṭākṣa-kiṅkarī-bhūta-kamalā-koṭi-sevitāyai
namaḥ 590
Oṁ śiraḥ-sthitāyai namaḥ
Oṁ candra-nibhāyai namaḥ
Oṁ bhālasthāyai namaḥ
Oṁ indra-dhanuṣ-prabhāyai namaḥ
Oṁ hṛdayasthāyai namaḥ
Oṁ ravi-prakhyāyai namaḥ
Oṁ tri-koṇānatara-dīpikāyai namaḥ
Oṁ dākṣāyaṇyai namaḥ
Oṁ daitya-hantryai namaḥ
Oṁ dakṣa-yajña-vināśinyai namaḥ 600
Oṁ dar'āndolita-dīrgh'ākṣyai namaḥ
Oṁ dara-hās'ojjvalan-mukhyai namaḥ
Oṁ guru-mūrtaye namaḥ
Oṁ guṇa-nidhaye namaḥ
Oṁ go-mātre namaḥ
Oṁ guha-janma-bhūve namaḥ
Oṁ deveśyai namaḥ
Oṁ daṇḍa-nītisthāyai namaḥ
Oṁ dahar'ākāśa-rūpiṇyai namaḥ
Oṁ pratipan-mukhya-rākānta-tithi-maṇḍala-pūjitāyai
namaḥ 610
Oṁ kal'ātmikāyai namaḥ
Oṁ kalā-nāthāyai namaḥ
Oṁ kāvy'ālāpa-vinodinyai namaḥ
Oṁ sacāmara-ramā-vāṇī-savya-dakṣiṇa-sevitāyai namaḥ
Oṁ ādiśaktyai namaḥ
Oṁ ameyāyai namaḥ

Oṁ ātmane namaḥ
Oṁ paramāyai namaḥ
Oṁ pāvan’ākṛtaye namaḥ
Oṁ aneka-koṭi-brahmāṇḍa-jananyai namaḥ 620
Oṁ divya-vigrahāyai namaḥ
Oṁ klīṅkāryai namaḥ
Oṁ kevalāyai namaḥ
Oṁ guhyāyai namaḥ
Oṁ kaivalya-pada-dāyinyai namaḥ
Oṁ tripurāyai namaḥ
Oṁ trijagad-vandyāyai namaḥ
Oṁ tri-mūrtaye namaḥ
Oṁ tridaś’eśvaryai namaḥ
Oṁ tryakṣaryai namaḥ 630
Oṁ divya-gandh’āḍhyāyai namaḥ
Oṁ sindūra-tilak’āñcitāyai namaḥ
Oṁ umāyai namaḥ
Oṁ śailendra-tanayāyai namaḥ
Oṁ gauryai namaḥ
Oṁ gandharva-sevitāyai namaḥ
Oṁ viśva-garbhāyai namaḥ
Oṁ svarṇa-garbhāyai namaḥ
Oṁ avaradāyai namaḥ
Oṁ vāg-adhīśvaryai namaḥ 640
Oṁ dhyāna-gamyāyai namaḥ
Oṁ apari-cchedyāyai namaḥ
Oṁ jñāna-dāyai namaḥ
Oṁ jñāna-vigrahāyạі namaḥ
Oṁ sarva-vedānta-saṁvedyāyai namaḥ
Oṁ saty’ānanada-svarūpiṇyai namaḥ
Oṁ lopāmudr’ārcitāyai namaḥ
Oṁ līlā-kḷpta-brahmāṇḍa maṇḍalāyai namaḥ
Oṁ adṛśyāyai namaḥ
Oṁ dṛśya-rahitāyai namaḥ 650
Oṁ vijñātryai namaḥ

Oṁ vedya-varjitāyai namaḥ
Oṁ yoginyai namaḥ
Oṁ yoga-dāyai namaḥ
Oṁ yogyāyai namaḥ
Oṁ yogānandāyai namaḥ
Oṁ yugandharāyai namaḥ
Oṁ icchā-śakti-jñāna-śakti-kriyā-śakti svarūpiṇyai namaḥ
Oṁ sarv'ādhārāyai namaḥ
Oṁ supratiṣṭhāyai namaḥ 660
Oṁ sad-asad-rūpa-dhāriṇyai namaḥ
Oṁ aṣṭa-mūrtyai namaḥ
Oṁ ajā-jetryai namaḥ
Oṁ loka-yātrā-vidhāyinyai namaḥ
Oṁ ekākinyai namaḥ
Oṁ bhūma-rūpāyai namaḥ
Oṁ nirdvaitāyai namaḥ
Oṁ dvaita-varjitāyai namaḥ
Oṁ annadāyai namaḥ
Oṁ vasudāyai namaḥ 670
Oṁ vṛddhāyai namaḥ
Oṁ brahm'ātmaikya-svarūpiṇyai namaḥ
Oṁ bṛhatyai namaḥ
Oṁ brahmāṇyai namaḥ
Oṁ brāhmyai namaḥ
Oṁ brahm'ānandāyai namaḥ
Oṁ bali-priyāyai namaḥ
Oṁ bhāṣā-rūpāyai namaḥ
Oṁ bṛhat-senāyai namaḥ
Oṁ bhāv'ābhāva-vivarjitāyai namaḥ 680
Oṁ sukh'ārādhyāyai namaḥ
Oṁ śubha-karyai namaḥ
Oṁ śobhanā-sulabhā-gatyai namaḥ
Oṁ rāja-rāj'eśvaryai namaḥ
Oṁ rājya-dāyinyai namaḥ
Oṁ rājya-vallabhāyai namaḥ

Oṁ rājat-kṛpāyai namaḥ
Oṁ rāja-pīṭha-niveśita-nijāśritāyai namaḥ
Oṁ rājya-lakṣmyai namaḥ
Oṁ kośa-nāthāyai namaḥ 690
Oṁ catur-aṅga-bal'eśvaryai namaḥ
Oṁ sāmrājya-dāyinyai namaḥ
Oṁ satya-sandhāyai namaḥ
Oṁ sāgara-mekhalāyai namaḥ
Oṁ dīkṣitāyai namaḥ
Oṁ daitya-śamanyai namaḥ
Oṁ sarva-loka-vaśaṅkaryai namaḥ
Oṁ sarvārtha-dātryai namaḥ
Oṁ sāvitryai namaḥ
Oṁ sac-cid-ānanda-rūpiṇyai namaḥ 700
Oṁ deśa-kāl'āparicchinnāyai namaḥ
Oṁ sarvagāyai namaḥ
Oṁ sarva-mohinyai namaḥ
Oṁ sarasvatyai namaḥ
Oṁ śāstra-mayyai namaḥ
Oṁ guhāmbāyai namaḥ
Oṁ guhya-rūpiṇyai namaḥ
Oṁ sarv'opādhi-vinirmuktāyai namaḥ
Oṁ sadāśiva-pativratāyai namaḥ
Oṁ sampradāy'eśvaryai namaḥ 710
Oṁ sādhune namaḥ
Oṁ yai namaḥ
Oṁ guru-maṇḍala-rūpiṇyai namaḥ
Oṁ kulottīrṇāyai namaḥ
Oṁ bhag'ārādhyāyai namaḥ
Oṁ māyāyai namaḥ
Oṁ madhumatyai namaḥ
Oṁ mahyai namaḥ
Oṁ gaṇāmbāyai namaḥ
Oṁ guhyak'ārādhyāyai namaḥ 720
Oṁ komalāṅgyai namaḥ

Oṁ guru-priyāyai namaḥ
Oṁ svatantrāyai namaḥ
Oṁ sarva-tantr'eśyai namaḥ
Oṁ dakṣiṇā-mūrti-rūpiṇyai namaḥ
Oṁ sanakādi-sam'ārādhyāyai namaḥ
Oṁ śiva-jñāna-pradāyinyai namaḥ
Oṁ cit-kalāyai namaḥ
Oṁ ānanda-kalikāyai namaḥ
Oṁ prema-rūpāyai namaḥ 730
Oṁ priyaṅkaryai namaḥ
Oṁ nāma-pārāyaṇa-prītāyai namaḥ
Oṁ nandi-vidyāyai namaḥ
Oṁ naṭ'eśvaryai namaḥ
Oṁ mithyā-jagad-adhiṣṭhānāyai namaḥ
Oṁ mukti-dāyai namaḥ
Oṁ mukti-rūpiṇyai namaḥ
Oṁ lāsya-priyāyai namaḥ
Oṁ laya-karyai namaḥ
Oṁ lajjāyai namaḥ
Oṁ rambh'ādi-vanditāyai namah 740
Oṁ bhava-dāva-sudhā-vṛṣṭyai namaḥ
Oṁ pāp'āraṇya-davānalāyai namaḥ
Oṁ daurbhāgya-tūla-vātūlāyai namaḥ
Oṁ jarā-dhvānta-ravi-prabhāyai namaḥ
Oṁ bhāgy'ābdhi-candrikāyai namaḥ
Oṁ bhakta-citta-keki-ghanā'ghanāyai namaḥ
Oṁ roga-parvata-dambholaye namaḥ
Oṁ mṛtyu-dāru-kuṭhārikāyai namaḥ
Oṁ mah'eśvaryai namaḥ 750
Oṁ mahā-kālyai namaḥ
Oṁ mahā-grāsāyai namaḥ
Oṁ mah'āśanāyai namaḥ
Oṁ aparṇāyai namaḥ
Oṁ caṇḍikāyai namaḥ
Oṁ caṇḍa-muṇḍāsura-niṣūdinyai namaḥ

Oṁ kṣar'ākṣar'ātmikāyai namaḥ
Oṁ sarva-lok'eśyai namaḥ
Oṁ viśva-dhāriṇyai namaḥ
Oṁ tri-varga-dātryai namaḥ 760
Oṁ subhagāyai namaḥ
Oṁ tryambakāyai namaḥ
Oṁ triguṇ'ātmikāyai namaḥ
Oṁ svarg'āpavarga-dāyai namaḥ
Oṁ śuddhāyai namaḥ
Oṁ japā-puṣpa-nibh'ākṛtyai namaḥ
Oṁ ojovatyai namaḥ
Oṁ dyuti-dharāyai namaḥ
Oṁ yajña-rūpāyai namaḥ
Oṁ priya-vratāyai namaḥ 770
Oṁ dur'ārādhyāyai namaḥ
Oṁ dur'ādharṣāyai namaḥ
Oṁ pāṭalī-kusuma-priyāyai namaḥ
Oṁ mahatyai namaḥ
Oṁ meru-nilayāyai namaḥ
Oṁ mandāra-kusuma-priyāyai namaḥ
Oṁ vīr'ārādhyāyai namaḥ
Oṁ virāḍ-rūpāyai namaḥ
Oṁ virajase namaḥ
Oṁ viśvato-mukhyai namaḥ 780
Oṁ pratyag-rūpāyai namaḥ
Oṁ par'ākāśāyai namaḥ
Oṁ prāṇa-dāyai namaḥ
Oṁ prāṇa-rūpiṇyai namaḥ
Oṁ mārtāṇḍa-bhairav'ārādhyāyai namaḥ
Oṁ mantriṇī-nyasta-rājya-dhure namaḥ
Oṁ tripur'eśyai namaḥ
Oṁ jayat-senāyai namaḥ
Oṁ nistraiguṇyāyai namaḥ
Oṁ par'āparāyai namaḥ 790
Oṁ satya-jñān'ānanda-rūpāyai namaḥ

Oṁ sāmarasya-parāyaṇāyai namaḥ
Oṁ kapardinyai namaḥ
Oṁ kalā-mālāyai namaḥ
Oṁ kāma-dughe namaḥ
Oṁ kāma-rūpiṇyai namaḥ
Oṁ kalā-nidhaye namaḥ
Oṁ kāvya-kalāyai namaḥ
Oṁ rasa-jñāyai namaḥ
Oṁ rasa-śevadhaye namaḥ 800
Oṁ puṣṭāyai namaḥ
Oṁ purātanāyai namaḥ
Oṁ pūjyāyai namaḥ
Oṁ puṣkarāyai namaḥ
Oṁ puṣkar'ekṣaṇāyai namaḥ
Oṁ parasmai jyotiṣe namaḥ
Oṁ parasmai dhāmne namaḥ
Oṁ param'āṇave namaḥ
Oṁ parāt-parāyai namaḥ
Oṁ pāśa-hastāyai namaḥ 810
Oṁ pāśa-hantryai namaḥ
Oṁ para-mantra-vibhedinyai namaḥ
Oṁ mūrtāyai namaḥ
Oṁ amūrtāyai namaḥ
Oṁ anitya-tṛptāyai namaḥ
Oṁ muni-mānasa-hamsikāyai namaḥ
Oṁ satya-vratāyai namaḥ
Oṁ satya-rūpāyai namaḥ
Oṁ sarv'āntar-yāmiṇyai namaḥ
Oṁ satyai namaḥ 820
Oṁ brahmāṇyai namaḥ
Oṁ brahmaṇe namaḥ
Oṁ jananyai namaḥ
Oṁ bahu-rūpāyai namaḥ
Oṁ budh'ārcitāyai namaḥ
Oṁ prasavitryai namaḥ

Oṁ pracaṇḍāyai namaḥ
Oṁ ājñāyai namaḥ
Oṁ pratiṣṭhāyai namaḥ
Oṁ prakaṭ'ākṛtaye namaḥ 830
Oṁ prāṇ'eśvaryai namaḥ
Oṁ prāṇa-dātryai namaḥ
Oṁ pañcāśat-pīṭha-rūpiṇyai namaḥ
Oṁ viśṛṅkhalāyai namaḥ
Oṁ vivikta-sthāyai namaḥ
Oṁ vīra-mātre namaḥ
Oṁ viyat-prasuve namaḥ
Oṁ mukundāyai namaḥ
Oṁ mukti-nilayāyai namaḥ
Oṁ mūla-vigraha-rūpiṇyai namaḥ 840
Oṁ bhāva-jñāyai namaḥ
Oṁ bhava-rogaghnyai namaḥ
Oṁ bhava-cakra-pravartinyai namaḥ
Oṁ chandaḥ-sārāyai namaḥ
Oṁ śāstra-sārāyai namaḥ
Oṁ mantra-sārāyai namaḥ
Oṁ tal'odaryai namaḥ
Oṁ udāra-kīrtaye namaḥ
Oṁ uddāma-vaibhavāyai namaḥ
Om varṇa-rūpiṇyai namaḥ 850
Oṁ janma-mṛtyu-jarā-tapta-jana-viśrānti-dāyinyai namaḥ
Oṁ sarv'opaniṣad-udghuṣṭāyai namaḥ
Oṁ śāntyatīta-kal'ātmikāyai namaḥ
Oṁ gambhīrāyai namaḥ
Oṁ gagan'āntasthāyai namaḥ
Oṁ garvitāyai namaḥ
Oṁ gāna-lolupāyai namaḥ
Oṁ kalpanā-rahitāyai namaḥ
Oṁ kāṣṭhāyai namaḥ
Oṁ akāntāyai namaḥ 860
Oṁ kānt'ārdha-vigrahāyai namaḥ

Oṁ kārya-kāraṇa-nirmuktāyai namaḥ
Oṁ kāma-keli-taraṅgitāyai namaḥ
Oṁ kanat-kanaka-tāṭaṅkāyai namaḥ
Oṁ līlā-vigraha-dhāriṇyai namaḥ
Oṁ ajāyai namaḥ
Oṁ kṣaya-vinirmuktāyai namaḥ
Oṁ mugdhāyai namaḥ
Oṁ kṣipra-prasādinyai namaḥ
Oṁ antar-mukha-sam'ārādhyāyai namaḥ 870
Oṁ bahir-mukha-sudurlabhāyai namaḥ
Oṁ trayyai namaḥ
Oṁ trivarga-nilayāyai namaḥ
Oṁ tristhāyai namaḥ
Oṁ tripura-mālinyai namaḥ
Oṁ nir'āmayāyai namaḥ
Oṁ nir'ālambāyai namaḥ
Oṁ sv'ātm'ārāmāyai namaḥ
Oṁ sudhāsṛtyai namaḥ
Oṁ samsāra-paṅka-nirmagna-samuddharaṇa-paṇḍitāyai namaḥ 880
Oṁ yajña-priyāyai namaḥ
Oṁ yajña-kartryai namaḥ
Oṁ yajamāna-svarūpiṇyai namaḥ
Oṁ dharm'ādhārāyai namaḥ
Oṁ dhan'ādhyakṣāyai namaḥ
Oṁ dhana-dhānya-vivardhinyai namaḥ
Oṁ vipra-priyāyai namaḥ
Oṁ vipra-rūpāyai namaḥ
Oṁ viśva-brahmaṇa-kāriṇyai namaḥ
Oṁ viśva-grāsāyai namaḥ 890
Oṁ vidrum'ābhāyai namaḥ
Oṁ vaiṣṇavyai namaḥ
Oṁ viṣṇu-rūpiṇyai namaḥ
Oṁ ayonyai namaḥ
Oṁ yoni-nilayāyai namaḥ

Oṁ kūṭasthāyai namaḥ
Oṁ kula-rūpiṇyai namaḥ
Oṁ vīra-goṣṭhī-priyāyai namaḥ
Oṁ vīrāyai namaḥ
Oṁ naiṣkarmyāyai namaḥ 900
Oṁ nāda-rūpiṇyai namaḥ
Oṁ vijñāna-kalanāyai namaḥ
Oṁ kalyāyai namaḥ
Oṁ vidagdhāyai namaḥ
Oṁ baindav'āsanāyai namaḥ
Oṁ tattv'ādhikāyai namaḥ
Oṁ tattva-mayyai namaḥ
Oṁ tat-tvam-artha-svarūpiṇyai namaḥ
Oṁ sāma-gāna-priyāyai namaḥ
Oṁ somyāyai namaḥ 910
Oṁ sadāśiva-kuṭumbinyai namaḥ
Oṁ savy'āpasavya-mārgasthāyai namaḥ
Oṁ sarvāpad-vinivāriṇyai namaḥ
Oṁ svasthāyai namaḥ
Oṁ svabhāva-madhurāyai namaḥ
Oṁ dhīrāyai namaḥ
Oṁ dhīra-samarcitāyai namaḥ
Oṁ caitany'ārghya-samārādhyāyai namaḥ
Oṁ caitanya-kusuma-priyāyai namaḥ
Oṁ sadoditāyai namaḥ 920
Oṁ sadā-tuṣṭāyai namaḥ
Oṁ taruṇ'āditya-pāṭalāyai namaḥ
Oṁ dakṣiṇ'ādakṣiṇ'ārādhyāyai namaḥ
Oṁ dara-smera-mukh'āmbujāyai namaḥ
Oṁ kaulinī-kevalāyai namaḥ
Oṁ anarghya-kaivalya-pada-dāyinyai namaḥ
Oṁ stotra-priyāyai namaḥ
Oṁ stuti-matyai namaḥ
Oṁ śruti-samstuta-vaibhavāyai namaḥ
Oṁ manasvinyai namaḥ 930

Oṁ mānavatyai namaḥ
Oṁ mah'eśyai namaḥ
Oṁ maṅgalākṛtaye namaḥ
Oṁ viśva-mātre namaḥ
Oṁ jagad-dhātryai namaḥ
Oṁ viśālākṣyai namaḥ
Oṁ virāgiṇyai namaḥ
Oṁ pragalbhāyai namaḥ
Oṁ param'odārāyai namaḥ
Oṁ parā-modāyai namaḥ 940
Oṁ mano'mayyai namaḥ
Oṁ vyoma-keśyai namaḥ
Oṁ vimāna-sthāyai namaḥ
Oṁ vajriṇyai namaḥ
Oṁ vāmak'eśvaryai namaḥ
Oṁ pañca-yajña-priyāyai namaḥ
Oṁ pañca-preta-mañc'ādhi-śāyinyai namaḥ
Oṁ pañcamyai namaḥ
Oṁ pañca-bhūteśyai namaḥ
Oṁ pañca-saṅkhyo'pacāriṇyai namaḥ 950
Oṁ śāśvatyai namaḥ
Oṁ śāśvat'aiśvaryāyai namaḥ
Oṁ śarma-dāyai namaḥ
Oṁ śambhu-mohinyai namaḥ
Oṁ dharāyai namaḥ
Oṁ dhara-sutāyai namaḥ
Oṁ dhanyāyai namaḥ
Oṁ dharmiṇyai namaḥ
Oṁ dharma-vardhinyai namaḥ
Oṁ lok'ātītāyai namaḥ 960
Oṁ guṇ'ātītāyai namaḥ
Oṁ sarv'ātītāyai namaḥ
Oṁ śam'ātmikāyai namaḥ
Oṁ bandhūka-kusuma-prakhyāyai namaḥ
Oṁ bālāyai namaḥ

Oṁ līlā-vinodinyai namaḥ
Oṁ sumaṅgalyai namaḥ
Oṁ sukha-karyai namaḥ
Oṁ suveṣāḍhyāyai namaḥ
Oṁ suvāsinyai namaḥ 970
Oṁ suvāsiny'arcana-prītāyai namaḥ
Oṁ āśobhanāyai namaḥ
Oṁ śuddha-mānasāyai namaḥ
Oṁ bindu-tarpaṇa-santuṣṭāyai namaḥ
Oṁ pūrva-jāyai namaḥ
Oṁ tripur'āmbikāyai namaḥ
Oṁ daśa-mudrā-sam'ārādhyāyai namaḥ
Oṁ tripurāśrī-vaśaṅkaryai namaḥ
Oṁ jñāna-mudrāyai namaḥ
Oṁ jñāna-gamyāyai namaḥ 980
Oṁ jñāna-jñeya-svarūpiṇyai namaḥ
Oṁ yoni-mudrāyai namaḥ
Oṁ trikhaṇḍ'eśyai namaḥ
Oṁ triguṇāyai namaḥ
Oṁ ambāyai namaḥ
Oṁ trikoṇagāyai namaḥ
Oṁ anaghāyai namaḥ
Oṁ adbhuta-cāritrāyai namaḥ
Oṁ vāñchit'ārtha-pradāyinyai namaḥ
Oṁ abhyās'ātiśaya-jñātāyai namaḥ 990
Oṁ ṣaḍadhv'ātīta-rūpiṇyai namaḥ
Oṁ avyāja-karuṇā-mūrtaye namaḥ
Oṁ ajñāna-dhvānta-dīpikāyai namaḥ
Oṁ ābāla-gopa-viditāyai namaḥ
Oṁ sarv'ānullaṅghya-śāsanāyai namaḥ
Oṁ śrīcakra-rāja-nilayāyai namaḥ
Oṁ śrīmat-tripura-sundaryai namaḥ
Oṁ śrī-śivāyai namaḥ
Oṁ śiva-śakty'aikya-rūpiṇyai namaḥ
Oṁ lalitāmbikāyai namaḥ 1000

Dhyānam

sindūrāruṇa-vigrahāṁ tri-nayanām māṇikya mauli-sphurat
tārānāyaka-śekharām smitamukhīm āpīna-vakṣoruhām
pāṇibhyām alipūrṇa-ratna-caṣakam raktotpalam bibhratīm
saumyāṁ ratna-ghaṭastha-rakta caraṇāṁ dhyāyetparāmambikām

dhyāyet padmāsanasthām vikasita-vadanām
padma-patrāyatākṣīm
hemābhām pītavastrām kara-kalita-lasad
hema padmām varāṅgīm
sarvālaṅkāra-yuktām satatam-abhayadām
bhakta-namrām bhavānīm
śrīvidyām śāntamūrtim sakala-sura-nutāṁ
sarva sampat pradātrīm

sakuṅkuma-vilepanām alika-cumbi-kastūrikām
samanda-hasitekṣaṇām saśara-cāpa-pāśāṅkuśām
aśeṣa-jana-mohinīm aruṇa-mālya-bhūṣojvalām
japā-kusuma-bhāsurām japavidhau smaredambikām

aruṇāṁ karuṇā-taraṅgitākṣīṁ
dhṛta-pāśāṅkuśa-puṣpa-bāṇa-cāpām
aṇimādibhir āvṛtām mayūkhai
raham-ityeva vibhāvaye māheśīm

Śrī Lalitā Sahasranāma Stotram

Oṁ

Śrī-mātā śrī-mahā-rājñī
śrīmat simhāsan'eśvarī
cidagni-kuṇḍa-sambhūtā
deva-kārya-samudyatā 1

Udyad-bhānu-sahasrābhā
catur-bāhu-samạnvitā
rāga-svarūpa-pāśā ḍhyā
krodh'ākār'āṅkuś'ojjvalā 2

Mano-rūpekṣu-kodaṇḍā
pañca-tanmātra-sāyakā
nijāruṇa-prabhāpūra
majjad-brahmāṇḍa-maṇḍalā 3

Campak'āśoka-punnāga
saugandhika-lasat-kacā
kuruvinda-maṇi-śreṇī
kanat-koṭīra-maṇḍitā 4

Aṣṭamī-candra-vibhrāja
dalika-sthala-śobhitā
mukha-candra-kalaṅkābha
mṛga-nābhi-viśeṣakā 5

Vadana-smara-māṅgalya
gṛha-toraṇa-cillikā
vaktra-lakṣmī-parīvāha
calan-mīnābha-locanā 6

Nava-campaka-puṣpābha
nāsā-daṇḍa-virājitā
tārā-kānti-tiraskāri
nāsābharaṇa-bhāsurā 7

Kadamba-mañjarī-kḷpta
karṇa-pūra-manoharā
tāṭaṅka-yugalī-bhūta
tapanoḍupa-maṇḍalā 8

Padma-rāga śilādarśa
paribhāvi-kapolabhūḥ
nava-vidruma-bimba-śrī
nyakkāri-radana-cchadā 9

Śuddha vidy'āṅkur'ākāra
dvija-paṅkti-dvay'ojjvalā
karpūra-vīṭikāmoda
samākarṣi-digantarā 10

Nija-sallāpa-mādhurya
vinirbhartsita-kacchapī
manda-smita-prabhā-pūra
majjat-kāmeśa-mānasā 11

Anākalita-sādṛśya
cibuka-śrī-virājitā
kāmeśa-baddha-māṅgalya
sūtra-śobhita-kandharā 12

Kanak'āṅgada-keyūra
kamanīya-bhujānvitā
ratna-graiveya-cintāka
lola-muktā-phalānvitā 13

Kāmeśvara-prema-ratna
maṇi-pratipaṇa-stanī
nābhyāla-vāla-romāli
latā-phala-kuca-dvayī 14

Lakṣya-roma-latā-dhāratā
samunneya-madhyamā
stana-bhāra dalan-madhya
paṭṭa-bandha-vali-trayā 15

Aruṇāruṇa-kausumbha
vastra-bhāsvat-kaṭī-taṭī
ratna-kiṅkiṇikā-ramya
raśanā-dāma-bhūṣitā 16

Kāmeśa-jñāta-saubhāgya
mārda'voru-dvayānvitā
māṇikya-mukuṭ'ākāra
jānu-dvaya-virājitā 17

Indra-gopa-parikṣipta
smara-tūṇābha-jaṅghikā
gūḍha-gulphā kūrma-pṛṣṭha
jayiṣṇu-prapadānvitā 18

Nakha-dīdhiti-saṁchanna
namajjana-tamo-guṇā
pada-dvaya-prabhā-jāla
parākṛta-saroruhā 19

Siñjāna-maṇi-mañjīra
maṇḍita-śrī-padāmbujā
marālī-manda-gamanā
mahā-lāvaṇya-śevadhiḥ 20

Sarv'āruṇā navadyāṅgī
sarv'ābharaṇa-bhūṣitā
śiva-kāmeśvar'āṅkasthā
śivā svādhīna-vallabhā 21

Sumeru-madhya-śṛṅgasthā
śrīman-nagara-nāyikā
cintāmaṇi-gṛh'āntasthā
pañca-brahm'āsana-sthitā 22

Mahā-padmāṭavī-samsthā
kadamba-vana-vāsinī
sudhā-sāgara-madhyasthā
kāmākṣī kāmadāyinī 23

Devarṣi-gaṇa-saṅghāta
stūyamān'ātma-vaibhavā
bhaṇḍāsura-vadh'odyukta
śakti-senā-samanvitā 24

Sampatkarī-samārūḍha
sindhura-vraja-sevitā
aśvārūḍh'ādhiṣṭhit'āśva
koṭi-koṭibhir-āvṛtā 25

Cakra-rāja-rath'ārūḍha
sarv'āyudha-pariṣkṛtā
geya-cakra-rath'ārūḍha
mantriṇī parisevitā 26

Kiri-cakra rath'ārūḍha
daṇḍanāthā puraskṛtā
jvālā-mālinik'ākṣipta
vahni-prākāra-madhyagā 27

Bhaṇḍa-sainya-vadh'odyukta
śakti-vikrama-harṣitā
nityā-parākram'āṭopa
nirkṣaṇa-samutsukā 28

Bhaṇḍaputra-vadh'odyukta
bālā-vikrama-nanditā
mantriṇ'yambā-viracita
viṣaṅga-vadha-toṣitā 29

Viśukra-prāṇa-haraṇa
vārāhī-vīrya-nanditā
kāmeśvara-mukhāloka
kalpita-śrī-gaṇeśvarā 30

Mahā-gaṇeśa-nirbhinna
vighna-yantra-praharṣitā
bhaṇḍāsur'endra-nirmukta
śastra-pratyastra-varṣiṇī 31

Karāṅguli-nakhotpanna
nārāyaṇa-daśākṛtiḥ
mahā-pāśupat'āstrāgni
nirdagdh'āsura-sainikā 32

Kāmeśvar'āstra-nirdagdha
sabhaṇḍ'āsura śūnyakā
brahm'opendra-mahendr'ādi
deva-samstuta-vaibhavā 33

Hara-netr'āgni-sandagdha
kāma-sañjīvan'auṣadhiḥ
śrīmad-vāgbhava-kūṭaika
svarūpa-mukha-paṅkajā 34

Kaṇṭhādaḥ-kaṭi-paryanta
madhya-kūṭa-svarūpiṇī
śakti-kūṭ'aikat'āpanna
kaṭhy'adho-bhāga-dhāriṇī 35

Mūla-mantr'ātmikā-mūla
kūṭa-traya-kalebarā
kul'āmṛtaika-rasikā
kula-saṅketa-pālinī 36

Kulāṅganā kul'āntasthā
kaulinī kulayoginī
akulā samay'āntasthā
samay'ācāra-tatparā 37

Mūlādhāraika-nilayā
brahma-granthi-vibhedinī
maṇipūr'āntaruditā
viṣṇu-granthi-vibhedinī 38

Ājñā-cakr'āntarālasthā
rudra-granthi-vibhedinī
sahasrār'āmbuj'ārūḍhā
sudhā-sārābhi-varṣiṇī 39

Taḍil-latā-sama-ruciḥ
ṣaṭ-cakr'opari-samsthitā
mahā saktiḥ kuṇḍalinī
bisatantu-tanyasī 40

Bhavānī bhāvanāgamyā
bhavāraṇya-kuṭhārikā
bhadra-priyā bhadra-mūrtir
bhakta-saubhāgya-dāyinī 41

Bhakti-priyā bhakti-gamyā
bhakti-vaśyā bhay-āpahā
śāmbhavī śārad'ārādhyā
śarvāṇī śarma-dāyinī 42

Śāṅkarī śrīkarī sādhvī
śarac-candra-nibhānanā
śātodarī śāntimatī
nirādhārā nirañjanā 43

Nirlepā nirmalā nityā
nirākārā nirākulā
nirguṇā niṣkalā śāntā
niṣkāmā nirupaplavā 44

Nitya-muktā nirvikārā
niṣprapañcā nirāśrayā
nitya-śuddhā nitya-buddhā
niravadyā nirantarā 45

Niṣkāraṇā niṣkalaṅkā
nirupādhir-nirīśvarā
nīrāgā rāga-mathanī
nirmadā mada-nāśinī 46

Niścintā nirahaṅkārā
nirmohā moha-nāśinī
nirmamā mamatā-hantrī
niṣpāpā pāpa-nāśinī 47

Niṣkrodhā krodha-śamanī
nirlobhā lobha-nāśinī
niḥsamśayā samśaya-ghnī
nirbhavā bhava-nāśinī 48

Nirvikalpā nirābādhā
nirbhedā bheda-nāśinī
nirnāśā mṛtyu-mathanī
niṣkriyā niṣparigrahā 49

Nistulā nīla-cikurā
nirapāyā niratyayā
durlabhā durgamā durgā
duḥkha-hantrī sukha-pradā 50

Duṣṭadūrā durācāra
śamanī doṣa-varjitā
sarvajñā sāndra-karuṇā
samānādhika-varjitā 51

Sarva-śakti-mayī sarva
maṅgalā sad-gati-pradā
sarv'eśvarī sarva-mayī
sarva-mantra-svarūpiṇī 52

Sarva-yantr'ātmikā sarva
tantra-rūpā manonmanī
māh'eśvarī mahā-devī
mahā-lakṣmī mṛḍa-priyā 53

Mahā-rūpā mahā-pūjyā
mahā-pātaka-nāśinī
mahā-māyā mahā-sattvā
mahā-śaktir mahā-ratiḥ 54

Mahā-bhogā mah'aiśvaryā
mahā-vīryā mahā-balā
mahā-buddhir mahā-siddhir
mahā-yog'eśvar'eśvarī 55

Mahā-tantrā mahā-mantrā
mahā-yantrā mahāsanā
mahā-yāga-kram'ārādhyā
mahā-bhairava-pūjitā 56

Mah'eśvara-mahā-kalpa
mahā-taṇḍava-sākṣiṇī
mahā-kāmeśa-mahiṣī
mahā-tripura-sundarī 57

Catuṣ-ṣaṣṭ'yupacārāḍhyā
catuṣ-ṣaṣṭi-kalā-mayī
mahā-catuḥ-ṣaṣṭi-koṭi
yoginī-gaṇasevitā 58

Manu-vidyā candra-vidyā
candra-maṇḍala-madhyagā
cāru-rūpā cāru-hāsā
cāru-candra-kalā-dharā 59

Carācara-jagan-nāthā
cakra-rāja-niketanā
pārvatī padma-nayanā
padma-rāga-samaprabhā 60

Pañca-pretāsanāsīnā
pañca-brahma-svarūpiṇī
cinmayī paramānandā
vijñāna-ghana-rūpiṇī 61

Dhyāna-dhyātṛ-dhyeya-rūpā
dharmādharma-vivarjitā
viśva-rūpā jāgariṇī
svapantī taijasātmikā 62

Suptā prājñātmikā turyā
sarvāvasthā-vivarjitā
sṛṣṭi-kartrī brahma-rūpā
goptrī govinda-rūpiṇī 63

Samhāriṇī rudra-rūpā
tirodhāna-karīśvarī
sadāśiv'ānugraha-dā
pañca-kṛtya-parāyaṇā 64

Bhānu-maṇḍala-madhyasthā
bhairavī bhaga-mālinī
padm'āsanā bhagavatī
padma-nābha-sahodarī 65

Unmeṣa-nimiṣ'otpanna
vipanna-bhuvanāvalī
sahasra-śīṛsa-vadanā
sahasrākṣī sahasrapāt 66

Ābrahma-kīṭa-jananī
varṇāśrama-vidhāyinī
nij'ājñā-rūpa-nigamā
puṇy'āpuṇya-phala-pradā 67

Śruti-sīmanta-sindūrī
kṛta-pādābja-dhūlikā
sakal'āgama-sandoha
śukti-samputa-mauktikā 68

Puruṣārtha-pradā pūrṇā
bhoginī bhuvan'eśvarī
ambik'ānādi-nidhanā
hari-brahm'endra-sevitā 69

Nārāyaṇī nāda-rūpā
nāma-rūpa-vivarjitā
hrīṅkārī hrīmatī hṛdyā
hey'opādeya-varjitā 70

Rāja-rāj'ārcitā rājñī
ramyā rājīva-locanā
rañjanī ramaṇī rasyā
raṇat-kiṅkiṇi-mekhalā 71

Ramā rākendu-vadanā
rati-rūpā rati-priyā
rakṣā-karī rākṣa-saghnī
rāmā ramaṇa-lampaṭā 72

Kāmyā kāma-kalā-rūpā
kadamba-kusuma-priyā
kalyāṇī jagatī-kandā
karuṇā-rasa-sāgarā 73

Kalāvatī kalālāpā
kāntā kādambarī-priyā
varadā vāma-nayanā
vāruṇī-mada-vihvalā 74

Viśvādhikā veda-vedyā
vindhy'ācala-nivāsinī
vidhātrī veda-jananī
viṣṇu-māyā vilāsinī 75

Kṣetra-svarūpā kṣetreśī
kṣetra-kṣetrajña pālinī
kṣaya-vṛddhi-vinirmuktā
kṣetra-pāla-samarcitā 76

Vijayā vimalā vandyā
vandāru-jana-vatsalā
vāg-vādinī vāma-keśī
vahni-maṇḍala-vāsinī 77

Bhaktimat-kalpa-latikā
paśu-pāśa-vimocinī
samhṛt'āśeṣa-pāṣaṇḍā
sadācāra-pravartikā 78

Tāpa-tray'āgni-santapta
sam'āhlādana-candrikā
taruṇī tāpas'ārādhyā
tanu-madhyā tamopahā 79

Citis tat-pada lakṣy'ārthā
cid'eka-rasa-rūpiṇī
svātm'ānanda-lavī-bhūta
brahm'ādy'ānanda-santatiḥ 80

Parā pratyak-citī-rūpā
paśyantī para-devatā
madhyamā vaikharī-rūpā
bhakta-mānasa-hamsikā 81

Kām'eśvara-prāṇa-nāḍī
kṛtajñā kāma-pūjitā
śṛṅgāra-rasa-sampūrṇā
jayā jālandhara-sthitā 82

Oḍyāṇa-pīṭha-nilayā
bindu-maṇḍala-vāsinī
raho-yāga-kram'ārādhyā
rahas-tarpaṇa-tarpitā 83

Sadyaḥ-prasādinī viśva
sākṣiṇī sākṣi-varjitā
ṣaḍ-aṅga-devatā-yuktā
ṣāḍ-guṇya-paripūritā 84

Nitya-klinnā nirupamā
nirvāṇa-sukha-dāyinī
nityā-ṣoḍaśikā-rūpā
śrīkaṇṭh'ārdha-śarīriṇī 85

Prabhāvatī prabhā-rūpā
prasiddhā param'eśvarī
mūla-prakṛtir avyaktā
vyakt'āvyakta-svarūpiṇī 86

Vyāpinī vividh'ākārā
vidy'āvidyā-svarūpiṇī
mahā-kāmeśa-nayana
kumud'āhlāda-kaumudī 87

Bhakta-hārda-tamo-bheda
bhānumaṭ-bhānu-santatiḥ
śiva-dūtī śiv'ārādhyā
śiva-mūrtiḥ śivaṅkarī 88

Śiva-priyā śiva-parā
śiṣṭ'eṣṭā śiṣṭa-pūjitā
aprameyā svaprakāśā
mano-vācām-agocarā 89

Cicchaktiś cetanā-rūpā
jaḍa-śaktir jaḍ'ātmikā
gāyatrī vyāhṛtiḥ sandhyā
dvija-vṛnda-niṣevitā 90

Tatv'āsanā tatvamayī
pañca-koś'āntara-sthitā
niḥsma-mahimā nitya
yauvanā mada-śālinī 91

Mada ghūrṇita-raktākṣī
mada-pāṭala-gaṇḍa-bhūḥ
candana-drava-digdhāṅgī
cāmpeya-kusuma-priyā 92

Kuśalā komal'ākārā
kurukullā kul'eśvarī
kula-kuṇḍ'ālayā kaula
mārga-tatpara-sevitā 93

Kumāra-gaṇa-nāth'āmbā
tuṣṭiḥ puṣṭir matir dhṛtiḥ
śāntiḥ svasti-matī kāntir
nandinī vighna-nāśinī 94

Tejovatī tri-nayanā
lolākṣī-kāma-rūpiṇī
mālinī haṁsinī mātā
malay'ācala-vāsinī 95

Sumukhī nalinī subhrūḥ
śobhanā sura-nāyikā
kāla-kaṇṭhī kānti-matī
kṣobhiṇī sūkṣma-rūpiṇī 96

Vajr'eśvarī vāma-devī
vay'ovasthā-vivarjitā
siddh'eśvarī siddha-vidyā
siddha-mātā yaśasvinī 97

Viśuddhi-cakra-nilay'ā
rakta-varṇā tri'locanā
khaṭvāṅgādi-praharaṇā
vadan'aika-samanvitā 98

Pāyasānna-priyā tvaksthā
paśu-loka-bhayaṅkarī
amṛtādi-mahā-śakti
samvṛtā ḍākin'īśvarī 99

Anāhatābja-nilayā
śyāmābhā vadana-dvayā
damṣṭr'ojjval'ākṣa-mālādi
dharā rudhira-samsthitā 100

Kāla-rātryādi-śakty'augha
vṛtā snigdh'audana priyā
mahā-vīrendra-varadā
rākiṇyambā-svarūpiṇī 101

Maṇipūr'ābja-nilayā
vadana-traya-samyutā
vajrādik'āyudhopetā
ḍāmaryādibhir-āvṛtā 102

Rakta-varṇā māṁsa-niṣṭhā
guḍānna-prīta mānasā
samasta-bhakta-sukhadā
lākiny'ambā-svarūpiṇī 103

Svādhiṣṭhān'āmbuja-gatā
catur-vaktra-manoharā
śul'ādy'āyudha-sampannā
pīta-varṇ'āti-garvitā 104

Medo-niṣṭhā madhu-prītā
bandhiny'ādi-samanvitā
dadhy'ānn'āsakta-hṛdayā
kākinī-rūpa-dhāriṇī 105

Mūlādhār'āmbuj'ārūḍhā
pañca-vaktr'āsthi samsthitā
aṅkuśādi-praharaṇā
varadādi-niṣevitā 106

Mudg'audan'āsakta-cittā
sākiny'ambā-svarūpiṇī
ājñā-cakr'ābja-nilayā
śukla-varṇā ṣad-ānanā 107

Majjā-samsthā hamsa-vatī
mukhya-śakti-samanvitā
haridrān'naika-rasikā
hākinī-rūpa-dhāriṇī 108

Sahasra-dala-padmasthā
sarva-varṇ'opa-śobhitā
sarv'āyudha-dharā śukla
samsthitā sarvatomukhī 109

Sarvaudana-prīta-cittā
yākiny'ambā-svarūpiṇī
svāhā svadh'āmatir medhā
śruti smṛtir anuttamā 110

Puṇya-kīrtiḥ puṇya-labhyā
puṇya-śravaṇa-kīrtanā
pulomaj'ārcitā bandha
mocanī barbarālakā 111

Vimarśa-rūpiṇī vidyā
viyad-ādi- jagat-prasūḥ
sarva-vyādhi-praśamanī
sarva-mṛtyu-nivāriṇī 112

Agra-gaṇy'ācintya-rūpā
kali-kalmaṣa-nāśinī
kātyāyanī kāla-hantrī
kamalākṣa-niṣevitā 113

Tāmbūla-pūrita-mukhī
dāḍimī-kusuma-prabhā
mṛgākṣī mohinī mukhyā
mṛḍānī mitra-rūpiṇī 114

Nitya-tṛptā bhakta-nidhir
niyantrī nikhil'eśvarī
maitry'ādi-vāsanā-labhyā
mahā-pralaya-sākṣiṇī 115

Parāśaktiḥ parāniṣṭhā
prajñāna-ghana-rūpiṇī
mādhvī-pān'ālasā mattā
mātṛkā-varṇa-rūpiṇī 116

Mahā-kailāsa-nilayā
mṛṇāla-mṛdu-dorlatā
mahanīyā dayā-mūrtir
mahā-sāṁrājya-śālinī 117

Ātma-vidyā mahā-vidyā
śrī-vidyā kāma-sevitā
śrī-ṣoḍaś'ākṣarī-vidyā
trikūṭā kāma-koṭikā 118

Kaṭākṣa-kiṅkarī-bhūta
kamalā-koṭi-sevitā
śiraḥ-sthitā candra-nibhā
phālasth'endra-dhanuḥ-prabhā 119

Hṛdayasthā ravi-prakhyā
tri-koṇ'āntara-dīpikā
dākṣāyaṇī daitya-hantrī
dakṣa-yajña-vināśinī 120

Darāndolita-dīrghākṣī
dara-hā'sojjvalan-mukhī
guru-mūrtir guṇa-nidhir
go-mātā guha-janma-bhūḥ 121

Dev'eśī daṇḍa-nītisthā
dahar'ākāśa-rūpiṇī
pratipan-mukhya-rākānta
tithi-maṇḍala-pūjitā 122

Kal'ātmikā kalā-nāthā
kāvy'ālāpa-vinodinī
sacāmara-ramā-vāṇī
savya-dakṣiṇa-sevitā 123

Ādiśaktir'amey'ātmā
paramā pāvanā-kṛtiḥ
aneka-koṭi-brahmāṇḍa
jananī divya-vigrahā 124

Klīṅkārī kevalā guhyā
kaivalya-pada-dāyinī
tripurā trijagad-vandyā
tri-mūrtir tridaś'eśvarī 125

Tryakṣarī divya-gandhāḍhyā
sindūra-tilakāñcitā
umā śailendra-tanayā
gaurī gandharva-sevitā 126

Viśva-garbhā svarṇa-garbhā'
vara-dā vāg-adhīśvarī
dhyāna-gamyā'paricchedyā
jñāna-dā jñāna-vigrahā 127

Sarva-vedānta-samvedyā
saty'ānanda-svarūpiṇī
lopāmudr'ārcitā līlā'
kḷpta-brahmāṇḍa maṇḍalā 128

Adṛśyā dṛśya-rahitā
vijñātrī vedya-varjitā
yoginī yoga-dā yogyā
yog'ānandā yugandharā 129

Icchā-śakti-jñāna-śakti-
kriyā-śakti svarūpiṇī
sarvā-dhārā supra-tiṣṭhā
sad-asad-rūpa-dhāriṇī 130

Aṣṭa-mūrtir ajā-jetrī
loka-yātrā-vidhāyinī
ekākinī bhūma-rūpā
nirdvaitā dvaita-varjitā 131

Anna-dā vasu-dā vṛddhā
brahm'ātmaikya-svarūpiṇī
bṛhat brahmāṇī brāhmī
brahm'ānandā bali-priyā 132

Bhāṣā-rūpā bṛhat-senā
bhāvābhāva-vivarjitā
sukh'ārādhyā śubha-karī
śobhanā-sulabhā-gatiḥ 133

Rāja-rāj'eśvarī rājya
dāyinī rājya-vallabhā
rājat-kṛpā rāja-pīṭha
niveśita-nijāśritā 134

Rājya-lakṣmīḥ kośa-nāthā
catur-aṅga-baleśvarī
sāmrājya-dāyinī satya
sandhā sāgara-mekhalā 135

Dīkṣitā daity'aśamanī
sarva-loka-vaśaṅkarī
sarvārtha-dātrī sāvitrī
sac-cid-ānanda-rūpiṇī 136

Deśa-kālāparic-chinnā
sarvagā sarva-mohinī
sarasvatī śāstramayī
guhāmbā guhya-rūpiṇī 137

Sarv'opādhi-vinirmuktā
sadāśiva-pativratā
sampradāy'eśvarī sādhvī
guru-maṇḍala-rūpiṇī 138

Kulottīrṇā bhag'ārādhyā
māyā madhumatī mahī
gaṇ'āmbā guhyak'ārādhyā
komal'āṅgī guru-priyā 139

Svatantrā sarva-tantreśī
dakṣiṇā-mūrti-rūpiṇī
sanakādi-sam'ārādhyā
śiva-jñāna-pradāyinī 140

Cit-kalānanda-kalikā
prema-rūpā priyaṅkarī
nāma-pārāyaṇa-prītā
nandi-vidyā naṭeśvarī 141

Mithyā-jagad-adhiṣṭhānā
mukti-dā mukti-rūpiṇī
lāsya-priyā laya-karī
lajjā rambhādi-vanditā 142

Bhava-dāva-sudhā-vṛṣṭiḥ
pāp'āraṇya-davānalā
daurbhāgya-tūla-vātūlā
jarā-dhvāntara-viprabhā 143

Bhāgy'ābdhi-candrikā bhakta
citta-keki-ghanāghanā
roga-parvata-dambholir
mṛtyu-dāru-kuṭhārikā 144

Maheśvarī mahā-kālī
mahā-grāsā mahāśanā
aparṇā caṇḍikā caṇḍa
muṇḍāsura-niṣūdinī 145

Kṣar'ākṣar'ātmikā sarva
lok'eśī viśva-dhāriṇī
tri-varga-dātrī subhagā
tryambakā triguṇ'ātmikā 146

Svarg'āpavarga-dā śuddhā
japā-puṣpa-nibhākṛtiḥ
ojovatī dyuti-dharā
yajña-rūpā priya-vratā 147

Dur'ārādhyā dur'ādharṣā
pāṭalī-kusuma-priyā
mahatī meru-nilayā
mandāra-kusuma-priyā 148

Vīr'ārādhyā virāḍ-rūpā
virajā viśvato-mukhī
pratyag-rūpā parākāśā
prāṇa-dā prāṇa-rūpiṇī 149

Mārtāṇḍa-bhairav'ārādhyā
mantriṇī-nyasta-rājya-dhūḥ
tripureśī jayat-senā
nistraiguṇyā parāparā 150

Satya-jñān'ānanda-rūpā
sāmarasya-parāyaṇā
kapardinī kalā-mālā
kāma-dhuk kāma-rūpiṇī 151

Kalā-nidhiḥ kāvya-kalā
rasa-jñā rasa-śevadhiḥ
puṣṭā purātanā pūjyā
puṣkarā puṣkar'ekṣaṇā 152

Param-jyotiḥ param-dhāma
param'āṇuḥ parāt-parā
pāśa-hastā pāśa-hantrī
para-mantra-vibhedinī 153

Mūrt'amūrt'ānitya-tṛptā
muni-mānasa-hamsikā
satya-vratā satya-rūpā
sarv'āntar-yāminī satī 154

Brahmāṇī brahma-jananī
bahu-rūpā budh'ārcitā
prasavitrī pracaṇḍājñā
pratiṣṭhā prakaṭākṛtiḥ 155

Prāṇ'eśvarī prāṇa-dātrī
pañcāśat-pīṭha-rūpiṇī
viśṛṅkhalā viviktasthā
vīra-mātā viyat-prasūḥ 156

Mukundā mukti-nilayā
mūla-vigraha-rūpiṇī
bhāva-jñā bhava-rogaghnī
bhava-cakra-pravartinī 157

Chandaḥ-sārā śāstra-sārā
mantra-sārā talodarī
udāra-kīrtir uddāma
vaibhavā varṇa-rūpiṇī 158

Janma-mṛtyu-jarā-tapta
jana-viśrānti-dāyinī
sarv'opaniṣad-udghuṣṭā
śānty'atīta-kalātmikā 159

Gambhīrā gaganāntasthā
garvitā gāna-lolupā
kalpanā-rahitā kāṣṭh'ā
kāntā kānt-ārdha-vigrahā 160

Kārya-kāraṇa-nirmuktā
kāma-keli-taraṅgitā
kanat-kanaka-tāṭaṅkā
līlā-vigraha-dhāriṇī 161

Ajā kṣaya-vinirmuktā
mugdhā kṣipra-prasādinī
antar-mukha-samārādhyā
bahir-mukha-sudurlabhā 162

Trayī trivarga-nilayā
tristhā tripura-mālinī
nirāmayā nirālambā
svātm'ārāmā sudhās'ṛtiḥ 163

Samsāra-paṅka-nirmagna
samuddharaṇa-paṇḍitā
yajña-priyā yajña-kartrī
yajamāna-svarūpiṇī 164

Dharm'ādhārā dhan'ādhyakṣā
dhana-dhānya-vivardhinī
vipra-priyā vipra-rūpā
viśva-brahmaṇa-kāriṇī 165

Viśva-grāsā vidrum'ābhā
vaiṣṇavī viṣṇu-rūpiṇī
ayonir yoni-nilayā
kūṭasthā kula-rūpiṇī 166

Vīra-goṣṭhī-priyā vīrā
naiṣkarmyā nāda-rūpiṇī
vijñāna-kalanā kalyā
vidagdhā baindav'āsanā 167

Tattvādhikā tattva-mayī
tat-tvam-artha-svarūpiṇī
sāma-gāna-priyā somyā
sadāśiva-kuṭumbinī 168

Savy'āpasavya-mārgasthā
sarv'āpad-vinivāriṇī
svasthā svabhāva-madhurā
dhīrā dhīra-samarcitā 169

Caitany'ārghya-samārādhyā
caitanya-kusuma-priyā
sad-oditā sadā-tuṣṭā
taruṇ-āditya-pāṭalā 170

Dakṣiṇ'ādakṣiṇārādhyā
dara-smera-mukhāmbujā
kaulinī-keval'ānarghya
kaivalya-pada-dāyinī 171

Stotra-priyā stuti-matī
śruti-samstuta-vaibhavā
manasvinī mānavatī
maheśī maṅgal'ākṛtiḥ 172

Viśva-mātā jagad-dhātrī
viśālākṣī virāgiṇī
pragalbhā param'odārā
parāmodā manomayī 173

Vyoma-keśī vimānasthā
vajriṇī vāmakeśvarī
pañca-yajña-priyā pañca
preta-mañc'ādhi-śāyinī 174

Pañcamī pañca-bhūteśī
pañca-saṅkhyopacāriṇī
śāśvatī śāśvat'aiśvaryā
śarma-dā śambhu-mohinī 175

Dharā dhara-sutā dhanyā
dharmiṇī dharma-vardhinī
lok'ātītā guṇ'ātītā
sarv'ātītā śam'ātmikā 176

Bandhūka-kusuma-prakhyā
bālā līlā-vinodinī
sumaṅgalī sukha-karī
suveṣāḍhyā suvāsinī 177

Suvāsinyarcana-prītā'
śobhanā śuddha'mānasā
bindu-tarpaṇa-santuṣṭā
pūrva-jā tripur'āmbikā 178

Daśa-mudrā-samārādhyā
tripurāśrī-vaśaṅkarī
jñāna-mudrā jñāna-gamyā
jñāna-jñeya-svarūpiṇī 179

Yoni-mudrā trikhaṇḍeśī
triguṇ'āmbā trikoṇagā
anagh'ādbhuta-cāritrā
vāñchit'ārtha-pradāyinī 180

Abhyās-ātiśaya-jñātā
ṣaḍadhv'ātīta-rūpiṇī
avyāja-karuṇā-mūrtir
ajñāna-dhvānta-dīpikā 181

Ābāla-gopa-viditā
sarv'ānullaṅghya-śāsanā
śrīcakra-rāja-nilayā
śrīmat-tripura-sundarī 182

Śrī-śivā śiva-śaktyaikya-rūpiṇī lalitāmbikā

Iti śrī brahmāṇḍa-purāṇe uttara-khaṇḍe
śrī hayagrīv'āgastya samvāde
śrī lalitā-sahasranāma stotra-kathanam sampūrṇam

Pronunciation Guide

TO CHANT in Sanskrit is to let the tongue dance against the roof of the mouth.

There are five mouth positions in Sanksrit. These are the throat, the soft palate, the roof of the mouth, the back of the front teeth, and the lips. Forty-nine letters of the alphabet are grouped according to these mouth positions, or where the tongue contacts the roof of the mouth when they are spoken. Sounds are referred to respectively as being gutteral, palatal, cerebral, dental, and labial, or *kānthya*, *tālavya*, *mūrdhanya*, *dantya*, and *oṣṭhya*.

In Sanskrit transliteration, diacritical marks identify a letter as being spoken with the tongue in contact with one of these five parts of the mouth. Commonly seen, a dot below a letter signifies that it is cerebral. It is spoken with the tip of the tongue touching the roof of the mouth. This type of marking is often seen with the consonants *t* or *d*. No marking implies the dental pronunciation of the *t* or *d* sound, or what we may think of as the common English pronunciation, with the tongue behind the front teeth. (Note: A dot below the *h* as in *namaḥ* signifies simply that the *h* is a vowel rather than a semivowel. It implies no change in pronunciation.)

In terms of vowel sound, some are short, while others are long. A line above a vowel signifies that it is a long vowel. It is held for an extra beat or *mātrā*.

Sibilants, or *s* sounds, may be palatal, cerebral, or dental. This is shown with an accent over the palatal *s* (ś), a dot beneath the cerebral *s* *(ṣ)*, and no marking on the dental *s*.

Nasal or *n* sounds may also be gutteral, palatal, cerebral, dental, or, if it is the sound *m*, labial. A gutteral *n* has a dot above it *(ṅ)*. A palatal *n* has a squiggle across the top *(ñ)*. A cerebral n has a dot beneath it *(ṇ)*. Dental *n* and labial *m* need no marking.

Of course, sound depends not only on the dance of the tongue but also on the breath. All sound except the unstruck *nādam* arises from the breath. So it is said that the Goddess births the alphabet in a single breath.

A brief and approximate pronunciation guide follows:

a	uh as in other
ā	aah as in olive (long)
i	i as in silly
ī	ee as in trapeze (long)
u	u as in push
ū	oo as in soothe (long)
e	ay as in eight
ai	eye as in either (long)
o	o as in over
au	ow as in allow (long)
ṅ	nga (gutteral)
ñ	nya (palatal)
ṇ	na (cerebral)
n	na (dental)
m	ma (labial)
ś	sha as in she (palatal)
ṣ	sha as in sugar (cerebral)
s	sa as in smart (dental)

Paying attention to pronunciation engages the mind. As we focus on each *mantra*, we let go of other thoughts. We become one-pointed, or *ekāgrata*. So, we are absorbed by the source of the *mantra*, the source of being.

That said, don't worry about chanting with perfect pronunciation. Enjoy the feeling and the sound of the syllables. It is well-known amongst the sages that if we take one step towards God, God will take nine-hundred-and-ninety-nine towards us. This is the nature of grace.

As I learned it, the chanting of the *Śrī Lalitā Sahasranāma* closes with the following lines:

mantra-hīnaṁ kriyā-hīnaṁ bhakti-hīnaṁ mahesvarī
yad-pūjitaṁ mayā devī paripūrṇaṁ tadāstute

In this offering, I may have made mistakes. I may have left out *mantras*, or not been properly devotional. Through your grace, please accept this offering and make it complete.

EPILOGUE:

Lord Siva's Poem for the Goddess

Lord Siva appears. It is not a dream.

Not Lord Krishna, though how long I have called him in song.

Lord Siva appears.

Truly will you know yourself with the poem written to you.
Not to me. To you. The reader.
You will know yourself to be the Goddess. She who is beyond name and form, time and space.

She is in everything, and yet, She does not truly exist.
Still, know yourself to be She.

You will overcome the fears and insecurities. The lingering self-doubt. The secret self-deprecation.

Leave them behind as you read Lord Siva's poem to you. It was written for you, for this purpose.

Siva Nilakantha. He who swallowed poison for the sake of the world. I am He and He is me.

Now, Lord Siva says, *I have written this poem to praise you. I am your eternal Beloved. Be still, and know me to be your own Self.*

Lord Siva's Poem for the Goddess

You are the Mother of all.
You are the great queen.
You sit astride the lion.
Born from the firepit of consciousness, you have come
to light the world.
Brighter are you than a thousand suns.
Like its rays, your reach extends in all directions.
I am bound only by your love.
Your anger is a paradox, for as you goad, you smile.
You turn the mind, like a bow of sweet sugarcane,
in any direction you please.
Direct all senses inward, for they are your arrows.
You are like the sunrise, flooding the universe
with your rosy glow.
I will intertwine your hair with flowers.
I offer you a brilliantly jeweled crown.
Your forehead glows like a half-moon.
You wear the musk smudge *bindi* like a dark spot on the moon.
Your eyebrows arch like doorways to the shining abode of love
that is your eyes.
They dart and glint in the stream of beauty that is your face.
Your nose is a budding flower.
You wear a diamond nose-stud that shines like a star
in the dark beauty of your face.
You are fascinating, as you tuck forest flowers behind your ears.
I offer the sun and the moon to you as earrings.
Your cheeks are more lustrous than rubies.
Your lips shine like freshly cut fruit.
Your teeth glow like pearls.

Your breath intoxicates the seeker with the scent
of fragrant betel leaf you chew.
The world is lost in the melodious tones of your voice.
Your smile absorbs the mind.
Your chin is shapely beyond compare.
As the One who is beyond desire, I tie the marriage thread
around your neck.
Your upper arms glitter with golden bangles.
Your necklace is strung with a locket of pearl, as well as myriad
gemstones and crystals, all equally precious to you.
One who worships you truly loves.
Your breasts hang above your navel like ripe fruit on the vine.
Your waist is barely visible.
Your abdomen has soft folds, as though a golden belt were wound
three times around the flesh of your belly.
You tie a scarf, red as sunrise, around your hips.
You wear jewels and tinkling bells beneath your skirts.
Your soft white thighs are for the touch of light alone.
Your ruddy knees are like crowns of precious ruby.
Your calves shine like a jeweled quiver.
Your ankles are ever hidden in modesty.
Your feet arch like the back of a tortoise.
Your toenails shine with such brilliance as to enlighten all
who take refuge at your feet.
Your feet surpass the lotus flower as a symbol of truth.
The sweet music of your jeweled anklets rings as the eternal *omkara*
for all who surrender to you.
You move with the grace of a floating swan.
Your beauty bends imagination.
You are robed in red silk.
Your limbs are flawless.
You are radiant, wearing all types of ornaments from head to toe.
You sit in the lap of the world like a child.
You absorb the world into silence.
The world yields to your wishes, like a beloved husband.

You live on the central peak of Mount Meru, the abode of the gods,
yet you dwell in the heart.
You are filled with the power of all worlds and beyond.
You live in a palace of gemstone that fulfills all wishes.
You sit upon a throne of five gods, four down on bended knee
to support me, the One who holds you.
You live in the great lotus forest of silence.
You dwell in a forest of flowering *kadamba* trees, their blossoms
infinite, like your love and wisdom.
You float on the ocean of bliss.
Your eyes entice the seeker to abandon worldly desires.
You satisfy the ultimate desire for freedom.
You are the refuge for innumerable gods and sages.
You lead an army to slay the demons of ignorance.
You tame the senses like a herd of wild elephants.
You command millions of untamed horses as your cavalry.
You wield weapons yet to be imagined, as you ride to glory
atop a nine-tiered chariot of bliss.
The sun rises and sets only to please you.
You hold death at bay.
You are the essence of fire.
You give strength to those who wage war with desire.
You are the strength and discipline of daily practice.
You delight in the dissolution of time.
You are the antidote to the seductive poisons of the world.
You uplift those who cling to sorrow.
Your sweet glance removes all obstacles.
You take joy in encouraging those grown tired.
You effortlessly deflect delusion.
You support the universe with your fingertips.
You offer delusion like grains of rice into the fire of wisdom.
You burn ignorance to blessed ash.
Your unfathomable power is praised by all.
You give new life to love.
Your face glows with the subtle power of *mantra*.

You fulfill worldly desires, so that the seeker may move
beyond them.
You guard the dormant power of bliss.
You embody the vibration of *mantra*.
Your subtle form contains all *mantra*.
You savor the bliss of union, as one might sip nectar.
You protect tradition.
You are of noble birth.
You rest in the essence.
You are the crown lotus of silence.
You rise through the seven *cakras*.
You love all beings as adorable children.
You reside as adoration in the heart of the seeker.
You hold inner worship to be the highest *sadhana*.
You rise from the root *cakra*, the seat of basic need.
You transcend instinct and urge.
You rise with confidence.
You unravel the knot of the heart.
You rest in the seat of wisdom.
You break through the last barrier to bliss.
You rise to the thousand-petaled lotus.
You merge with all in a rain of nectar.
Your beauty is as blinding as a flash of lightning in the night sky.
You are ever in union.
You are the radiant power of love.
You are the rising spiral of light.
You are delicate yet strong, like the lotus petal.
You are the desire for union and its fulfillment.
Your beauty is beyond language.
You cut through the jungle of suffering with ease,
as if you were a small, sharp axe.
You delight in both material and spiritual wealth.
You are the greatest treasure.
You bless all who love you with abundance.
You adore devotion.

You respond easily to devotion.
You are charmed by sincerity.
You protect those who love you from all fear.
You are the Mother to all who seek fulfillment.
You are praised by Sarada, the Goddess of wisdom.
You are the Mother of the earth.
You bestow worldly happiness.
You bless the seeker with everlasting bliss.
You support all life with your wealth.
You can be touched by light alone.
Your face shines like the brightest autumn moon.
Your waist is slender.
You are at peace.
You are self-reliant.
You cannot be bound by desire.
Your actions are beyond intention.
You remain free of impurity.
You transcend time.
You are not bound by form.
You know no agitation.
You are free of the tangled qualities of nature.
You are indivisible.
You are tranquil.
You are undisturbed by desire.
You shine in the face of disaster.
You are eternally free.
You witness the ongoing cycle of birth and rebirth.
You have created earth, water, fire, air, and space.
You are self-sustaining.
You are forever pure.
Your wisdom transcends time and space.
You are without fault.
You are the only fulfillment.
You are without cause, for you are the cause of all.
You are sinless, and so eradicate sin.

You are beyond body and mind.
You are the Lord.
You know no personal preference.
You churn wisdom from the seeker's desires.
You are not intoxicated by pride.
You nurture those who are humble.
You are free from anxiety.
You master the ego.
You see through the enchantment of the senses.
You cut through delusion for those who seek ruth.
You call nothing your own.
You root out selfishness in the seeker.
You are ever without sin.
You bring the seeker beyond sin.
You do not truly anger.
You soothe the seeker's anger.
You are without greed.
You free the seeker from the bondage of greed.
You know no doubt.
You relieve doubt in seekers and skeptics alike.
You know no becoming, for you are pure being.
You free all from the changes that are the cycle of birth and death.
You are never false.
You are beyond illusion.
You know all beings to be the essence of yourself.
You free the seeker from the pain of separation.
You are indestructible.
You are unborn, and so will never die.
You are the stillness from which action arises.
You accept with grace all that is offered, though you retain
nothing for yourself.
You know no equal, for you are one with all.
Your curls are dark and shining.
You are the essence that exists throughout the cycles of creation.
You are unchanging.

You may be difficult to attain.
You must be approached with patience.
You are the demon-slayer called Durga.
You eradicate sorrow.
You bestow only joy.
You hold no interest for those distracted by evil.
You redirect the distracted mind.
You are without harmful tendency.
You are omniscient.
You overflow with compassion.
You are indivisible, and so know none to be equal, inferior,
  or superior.
You are the wellspring of blessings.
You illuminate the path of truth.
You are the Lord of all.
All exists in you.
You are cosmic vibration.
You are sacred symbol.
You are ritual worship.
You are consciousness.
You are the soul of the worlds.
You are the great shining one.
You have taken form as the goddess Laksmi
  to preserve the universe and bestow prosperity.
You are the eternal beloved.
Your forms are great.
All worship you, in one form or another.
You uplift those ensnared by the world.
You weave the web of illusion.
You dispel that illusion.
You are the power of the universe.
You bestow delight beyond what is sensual.
You bestow the bliss of liberation.
You rule being, non-being, and beyond.
You are the greatest strength.

You are mighty.
You are the seat of wisdom.
You manifest the power of transformation.
You are the bliss of the *yogi*.
You are ritual, the object of worship,
and the power awakened by sacrifice.
You are the sound current of creation.
Your power is painted as *yantra*.
You are the seat of union.
You inspire sacrifice.
All offerings are offerings to you.
You are bear witness to the great dance,
in which the universe is absorbed.
You are the queen of desire.
You are the beautiful One who rules the city of light within.
You are adored in sixty-four different ways, from the washing
of your feet to the waving of the flame, and ultimately,
through complete surrender.
You flood the world with the beauty of sixty-four talents,
among them music, poetry, painting,
and the art of polite conversation.
You draw bands of *yoginis* in the number of sixty-four crores
to follow your example of purity.
For you, the gods and sages have created the twelve forms
of worship called *manuvidya*.
You are worshipped through one of these twelve called *candravidya*.
You shine at the center of the moon.
You are true beauty.
Your smile awakens the heart.
You wear the crescent moon in your crown.
You love all of creation.
You dwell in the innermost sanctum, *sricakra*.
You are Parvati, the daughter of the Himalaya Mountains.
Your eyes radiate love as they behold the world's suffering.
Your face, like a gemstone, reflects light in all directions.

You sit atop the forms of five who are powerless without you.
Your form subsumes these five.
You exist within and beyond all form.
You are the greatest bliss.
You are the wisdom that illuminates mind.
You are the state of meditation, as well as the meditator
and the object of meditation.
You act out of love alone, and so transcend ideas of right
and wrong.
The universe expands and contracts with your breath.
You are the waking state.
You are the dream state.
You are the body of light that lives in dreams.
You are the depths of sleep.
You are the soul that merges through deep sleep.
You are witness to the states of waking, dreaming, and deep sleep.
You transcend even this state of witness consciousness.
You create the universe to watch it evolve.
You take form as Brahma, the Creator.
You protect the universe.
You take form as the divine child cowherd.
You allow the universe to break down.
You bring tears, for sorrow purifies the heart just as rain
renews the earth.
You reabsorb your blessings, so that they appear to disappear.
You are Isvari, the consciousness of the universe.
You are eternal peace.
You spark the recreation of the universe.
You sustain the cycle of the universe.
You are the light of the sun.
You dance through the fires of cremation.
You wear blessings with humility,
as if they were a garland of fragrant flowers.
You are seated upon the lotus in full bloom.
You look upon all shortcomings with loving eyes.

You are like a sister to all.
The universe comes in and out of being with the blink of your eyes.
You are in the faces of all beings.
You have a thousand radiant eyes that are the stars, moons, suns, and sacrificial fires.
You move with the thousands of feet that cross the universe.
You are Mother to all beings, from the great Creator to the earthworm at your feet.
You structure society according to each being's innate tendencies.
Your commands are revered as scripture in the form of the Vedas.
You offer the fruit of each action in accordance with its merit or demerit.
The red dust of your feet decorates the foreheads of those wise goddesses, the Vedas incarnate, who prostrate to you.
You are the pearl of wisdom that shines from within the shell of scripture.
You bestow the fruits of human birth.
You are ever whole, even as you birth the universe.
You take pleasure in creation.
You are both the seed of creation and the ruler of the universe.
You are the Mother of the universe.
You are without beginning or end.
You are served by the gods Brahma and Hari, who create and support the world, as well as Indra who rules the heavens.
You take the form of sister to Narayana, who preserves the universe.
You are the subtle sound that pervades creation.
You are beyond name and form.
You speak the *mantra* that is the seed sound of creation, preservation, and transformation: *hrim*.
You are modestly robed in creation, and so known only to the pure of heart.
You reside in the hearts of all beings.
You desire no worldly pleasure, and so know neither attachment nor aversion.

You are worshipped by the king of kings.
You are the eternal queen.
You are delightful.
Your eyes are wide and bright like lotus flowers.
You are enchanting.
You are the one beloved.
You are the sap of bliss.
Your belt tinkles with tiny bells.
You are the soul of prosperity.
Your face is like the moon so full and bright that it shines
  by the light of day.
You embody love beyond desire.
You are the greatest pleasure.
You subdue the army of mental demons.
You are in all aspects feminine.
Never do you stray from truth.
You are eternally desired.
You are the marriage of the immanent soul
  to the transcendent spirit.
You are showered with handfuls of forest flowers, which you adore.
Your holy words water the heart.
You are the seed from which the universe blooms.
You are the ocean of nectar, the sea of compassion.
The arts bud forth from you like figs on a tree.
Your voice is musical.
You are pure beauty.
You savor the nectar of flowers.
You bestow freedom.
Your eyes flood the world with silence.
You are mad with the delight of bliss.
You live beyond the bounds of time and space.
You can be known through the Vedas.
You rule the Vindhya Mountains,
  for you have subdued their resident demons.
You offer eternal support.

You have brought forth the Vedas from your being,
as a mother births her children.
You are, at once, the truth and illusion of the universe.
You sport and play in the world of your creation.
You are the battlefield upon which truth conquers illusion.
You rule the field of creation.
You carefully protect both the field of action
and the one who knows it to be illusory.
You are eternally youthful.
You are worshipped by those born into your field of play.
You know no defeat.
You remain untainted by battle.
You are only to be adored.
You know all beings to be your darling children.
You are the origin of language.
Your hair is the midnight sky.
You are the light of sun, moon, and fire.
You are the flowering vine of the wishing tree.
You liberate the soul bound by animal desire.
You transform those who have turned from truth.
You inspire all to seek the eternal.
Like moonlight, you soothe those who burn in the fires
of purification.
You are ever the fair maiden.
You are the soul.
Your shape is like the hourglass that measures time.
You protect those bound by time.
You are free of time and space.
You light each being from within.
You cast the illusion of many forms
over the one bliss consciousness.
Brahma is but a drop in the ocean of your bliss.
You are the fulfillment of inner bliss.
You are unmanifested consciousness.
You are the rising of consciousness.

You are the merging of individual awareness with the highest bliss.
You unite beings of form with transcendent consciousness.
You are all words.
You are the swan of discrimination that floats
in the mind of the seeker.
You are the river of life.
You know all acts of desire.
You are the one who is worshipped.
You are adored as the full-blown flower of love.
You are victorious over desire.
You abide in the throat that swallows the world's poisons,
to redeem all beings for the love of you.
You rest in the sacred seat of intuition.
You dwell in the innermost shrine.
You are that secret inner sacrifice known only to pure seekers.
You are pleased by those who seek no glory from their worship.
You shower such a seeker with sudden grace.
You witness all workings of the worlds.
You transcend the witness consciousness.
You are one with all.
You are fulfillment.
You are eternal compassion.
You are beyond compare.
You bestow *nirvana.*
You are the essence of the sixteen eternal goddesses,
from Tripurasundari to Kamesvari.
You are the consciousness that takes both male and female form.
You are the light that pervades all.
Your form is luminous.
You are revered.
To your wishes, the wise bow.
You are the root cause of all that manifests in the natural world.
You are the imperishable force that supports the world.
You are the union of the manifest and unmanifest.
You pervade all.

You take innumerable forms.
You are both wisdom and ignorance.
You are like a water lily shining in the moonlight.
Your affections are like sunlight,
  dispelling the shadows of ignorance.
Transformation is your herald.
All offerings are made to you.
You are the body.
You confer the bliss of liberation.
You are endlessly adored.
You are more than free, for you have never been bound.
You are the beloved of the wise.
You are glorified by those who turn from fleeting pleasures.
Your love is immeasurable.
You are lit from within.
You absorb all thought and word.
You are the power of pure consciousness.
You are consciousness made manifest.
You are the workings of natural law.
You are the soul of inanimate being.
You are the one who saves.
You are the utterance of *mantra*.
You are the object of meditation.
You are to be adored at twilight.
You rest upon the subtle forces of the world.
You support the physical world.
You are transcendent reality and its appearance as creation.
To you, the soul cries out for union.
You are the five veils of the soul.
You transcend ideas of body, mind, and bliss.
You are the wellspring of youth and beauty.
You are in ecstasy beyond the worlds.
Your eyes roll upward with pleasure.
Your face is flushed with bliss.
Your limbs are adorned with fragrant sandal paste.

You are fond of the budding flowers that are offered at your feet.
You are skillful in all aspects of creation.
You act with grace throughout creation.
You lead the seeker from the desires of ego to pure consciousness.
You rule the river of consciousness as it flows ever upward.
You are seated at the source of this river.
You are worshipped by all who are selfless.
You are Mother to those bound by the illusion of separation.
You are contentment.
You are the ripe and perfect fullness of being.
You are wisdom.
You are fortitude.
You are tranquility.
You absolve the seeker from sin.
You are the source of light.
You are joy.
You clear the path of obstacles.
You are the inner light of creation.
You are all-seeing.
You are all that can be desired.
You are garlanded as the beloved.
You are the sound of the breath.
You breathe life into all.
You dwell amongst the sandalwood groves of the Malaya Mountain.
Your face is sweet.
Your limbs are as soft as lotus petals.
Your eyebrows are pleasingly arched.
You are the source of all beauty.
You lead the gods.
You are the seeker's solace.
Your beauty is brilliant.
Your loveliness agitates the mind.
Your beauty is subtle.
You are the thunder in the heavens.
You are to be worshipped, always and in all ways.

You know neither childhood nor old age,
  for your heart is ever in the bloom of youth.
All power is at your command.
You are the greatest power.
You bring forth all power.
You are famed throughout the worlds
  that come in and out of being.
You reside in the throat *cakra* as the goddess Dakini.
As Dakini, you have a complexion of rosy bloom.
As Dakini, you are three-eyed, and so, all-seeing.
As Dakini, you bear a club to eradicate the ego.
As Dakini, your face radiates the light of transformation.
As Dakini, you are fond of sweet milk pudding.
As Dakini, you are the goddess of touch.
As Dakini, you are frightening to those who fear their own potential.
As Dakini, you rest in the sixteen-petaled lotus of the throat
  where sixteen goddesses attend you.
You are the goddess Dakini, the purified mind that dances
  in the limitless space of consciousness.
You reside in the heart *cakra* as the goddess Rakini.
As Rakini, you are black in color.
As Rakini, you offer two faces to the world, casting the illusion
  of duality.
As Rakini, you have gleaming tusks.
As Rakini, you wear your weapon, the discus, strung on a necklace.
As Rakini, you are bloodthirsty in slaying the ego.
As Rakini, you stand at the center of the twelve-petaled lotus
  where twelve attendants surround you.
As Rakini, you savor clarified butter whenever it is offered.
As Rakini, you are the strength of heroes.
You are the ever-benevolent Mother in the form of Rakini.
You reside in the center of power, behind the navel,
  as the goddess Lakini.
As Lakini, you show the world three faces, in the spirit of creation,
  preservation, and transformation.

As Lakini, you hold the dart, the thunderbolt, and the discus.
As Lakini, you sit in the center of the ten-petaled lotus,
with ten attendants.
As Lakini, you are the color of life blood.
As Lakini, you rule the transformation and desire of the flesh.
As Lakini, you are delighted by confections.
As Lakini, you bestow sweet joy upon those who worship.
You are the Mother of all in the form of Lakini.
You reside in the *cakra* of creation as the one who is called Kakini.
As Kakini, your faces are four, like the fruits of human birth:
wealth, pleasure, purity, and liberation.
As Kakini, you bear the trident, along with the noose
of binding love and the skull of the slain ego.
As Kakini, you shine with a golden hue.
As Kakini, you are dignified, strong, and beautiful.
As Kakini, you are the ruler of excess.
As Kakini, you adore offerings of dripping honey.
As Kakini, you are attended by six,
as you rule from the six-petaled lotus.
As Kakini, you cool your food with curd.
You are the essence of the form called Kakini.
You rise from the root *cakra* as the goddess Sakini.
As Sakini, you have five faces,
reflecting the five elements of the universe.
As Sakini, you rule inner structure.
As Sakini, you hold the elephant goad, the lotus, a book,
and *jnana mudra*, the seal of wisdom.
As Sakini, you are served by four from your seat,
the four-petaled lotus.
As Sakini, you savor the taste of *mudga* beans.
You are the Mother in the form of Sakini.
You reside in the seat of intuition, between the eyebrows,
as the goddess Hakini.
As Hakini, you are pure white in color.

As Hakini, your faces are six, like the senses,
  including the subtle sense of intuition.
As Hakini, you manifest as the innermost essence of form.
As Hakini, you keep two favored attendants by your side,
  as you sit upon the two-petaled lotus.
As Hakini, you adore the taste of saffron.
You take the form of Hakini.
You live in the eternal silence of the thousand-petaled lotus
  as the goddess Yakini.
As Yakini, you are resplendent, for you shine with all colors.
As Yakini, you hold weapons yet to be imagined in each
  of your thousand hands.
As Yakini, you are the source of creation.
As Yakini, you see in all directions: those marked by the compass,
  those beyond, and those within.
As Yakini, you find all food delectable,
  for you are beyond preference.
You are the Mother in the form of Yakini.
You are Vedic sacrifice, as well as the call of offering: *svaha.*
You are the sound that satisfies the spirit: *svadha.*
You have existed since before the first dawn.
You are the intelligence incipient in ignorance.
You are the song of scripture.
You are the remembrance of truth.
Your heart floods the universe with wisdom.
Your blessings are glorious.
You are known through the purity of your deeds.
Your name brings purity whenever it is praised.
You are worshipped as the one who upholds the heavens.
You free all from the prison of impure deeds.
Your dark locks flow down your back in waves.
You are the first vibration of light.
You are the power of discrimination
  between the real and the unreal.
You are the infinite love from which all beings are born.

You calm fears of illness and aging.
You live beyond death.
You are the first cause of all.
Your form outlasts the mind.
You purify the Iron Age of sin, as water quenches fire,
or as light dispels darkness.
You are the essence of light.
In your gaze, time is stilled.
Lotus-eyes worship you.
Your mouth is filled with betel leaf.
Your face is as bright as the pomegranate flower.
Your eyes are like a fawn's.
Your beauty silences the mind.
You are a natural leader.
Your rule gives happiness.
You are a friend to all.
You are eternal contentment.
You fulfill longing.
You are inner guidance.
You rule all that is, all that is not, and all that will come to be.
You bring peace of mind through your friendship.
You are the great dance, through which the universe is absorbed.
You are the power of creation and dissolution.
You are the dissolution of ignorance.
You are the form of pure knowledge.
Your limbs are as languid as the drunk's.
You are intoxicated by the wine of the heart.
You birth the alphabet in a single breath.
You abide in the ether that floats above Mount Kailas.
Your arms are as graceful as flowering vines.
You are adored by all.
You embody mercy.
You rule the universe sweetly, as if you were the mistress
of a modest home.
You are the knowledge of the soul.

You are devotion.
You are the great Goddess *mantra*, the *srividya* of fifteen syllables
that bestows the fruit of all *mantra*.
You are the formless beloved.
You are the truth of the *srividya mantra*, made sixteen-syllabled
for the pure seeker.
This *mantra* is your body, mind, and soul.
You bestow liberation from these three illusions.
You are attended by hosts of goddesses,
those who bestow all prosperity and bow at your very glance.
You are ever in the state of meditation.
You are the calm light of the moon.
You adorn the seeker's forehead as the *bindu*, the sacred syllable *hrim*.
You shine with all colors of the rainbow.
Your abode is the heart of all beings.
Your love is like sunlight.
You are the flame that lights the three worlds.
You are the one for whom the stars shine.
You root out evil tendencies.
Your love is the sacrificial fire.
Your gentle gaze dispels fear.
The world is lit by your smile.
You remove darkness.
You are the merciful ocean that dissolves all concept.
You are mother to the sacred cow.
Your children overcome all obstacles.
You are Lord of the gods.
You rule fairly.
You are the subtle self.
You are worshipped with the phases of the moon, from new to full.
You are all phases of the moon's cycle.
You are the cycle of birth and death.
Poetry is composed for your pleasure.
The goddesses of prosperity and wisdom tend to you
with long-handled fans.

You are the primal energy of the universe.
You know no bounds.
You are the soul.
You are supreme being.
You are purity.
You birth infinite worlds.
Your form is divine.
You are the seed sound of desire: *klim*.
You desire nothing, for you are all that is, has been, and ever will be.
You renounce the world, even as you move through it.
You bestow absolute bliss.
You rule all modes of trinity.
You are the merging of mind with heart.
You are worshipped in the three worlds and beyond.
You rule all forms of divinity.
You are the desire that yields to wisdom.
You are of divine fragrance.
You wear the mark of vermilion, like a rising sun on your forehead.
You are as delicate as a China rose.
You are the mountain princess.
You glow with a golden light.
You inspire the songs of angels.
You birth the universe from a golden egg.
You birth all from your shining womb.
You conquer all demons.
You preside over speech.
You are known when the mind is quiet.
You transcend space and time.
You grant wisdom beyond intelligence.
You are true knowledge.
You are the one whom the scriptures praise.
You are the blissful source of truth.
You are worshipped by women whose hearts are pure.
You birth and reabsorb the worlds, as if it were child's play.
You are the seer behind the eyes.

You transcend all that the eyes can see.
You know all that is to be known.
You transcend the knowledge of mind.
You are ever in union.
You bestow union upon the seeker.
You are the union of body, mind, and soul with pure consciousness.
You are the bliss of that union.
You are the love that unites myriad created beings as one
without beginning or end.
You are the power of desire, tempered by wisdom,
and offered as purity in action.
You are one with creation.
You are firmly rooted.
You exist throughout manifest and unmanifest existence.
Your forms are eight, like the limbs of *yoga*.
You dispel illusion.
The worlds come in and out of existence at your will.
You are unity.
You are all time.
You are beyond the duality of the manifest and unmanifest.
You absorb duality.
You feed the world.
You bestow prosperity.
You are the primordial giver of life.
You are the merging of created being with that which has no form.
You are vast.
Your wisdom is like a healing herb: the antidote
to the suffering of ignorance.
You have always been and will always be.
You are the ecstasy of union.
You receive the offering of true love.
You are the honeyed tone of the lover's voice.
You command powerful forces.
You neither are nor are not.
You bring no suffering to those who love you.

You bless those who err.
Your holy footsteps are easy to follow.
You rule great monarchs.
You bestow the crown of wisdom.
You are adored by those who rule.
You rule with compassion.
You raise servants to be kings.
You are the wealth of kings.
You part the five veils of the soul,
so that the soul may merge with truth.
You lead the world's armies—cavalry, infantry, chariots,
and elephants.
You bestow dominion in the three worlds and beyond.
You are one with truth.
You are Mother Earth, wearing the ocean as your girdle.
You live under holy vow.
You soothe the mind that is agitated by desire.
Your charm calms the three worlds.
You grant all wishes.
You create all that is desired.
You are the form of truth, consciousness, and bliss.
You are space.
You are everywhere.
You enchant all.
You are Sarasvati, the Goddess of wisdom.
From you, the sciences flow.
You light the cave of the heart.
You are the essence that is imperceptible to the senses.
You are free from the illusion of separation.
You are devoted to all beings, who are ever-absorbed in you.
You speak without words.
You purify.
You are the all-pervasive teaching.
You are the inner circle of devotees.
You break the bondage of sensory pleasure.

You are adored as the sun disc.
You are the power of illusion.
Your glance is like wild honey.
You cast the spell of illusion over the world.
You are Mother to truth-seekers.
To you, the gods bow.
Your limbs are soft.
You are the beloved of the *guru* who removes the shadows of ignorance.
You create all from within yourself.
You are inspiration.
You instruct the gods.
You are worshipped by all lineage.
You bestow the wisdom of silence.
You are consciousness come to life in the world.
You are the budding flower of bliss.
You embody pure love.
You arouse devotion.
You are pleased by the chanting of your names.
You are the power of wisdom.
You rule the dance of life.
You uphold the worlds that come in and out of existence.
You bestow liberation.
You are liberation in female form.
You abandon yourself to the dance.
You are the hush of beauty.
You are modest.
You are feminine lure.
You douse the fires of worldly desire in a rain of nectar.
You are the forest fire of purification.
You are the breeze that blows misfortune away.
You are like sunlight, dispelling the shadows of affliction.
You are the moonlight reflected in the ocean of bliss.
You are the rain cloud complexion of the one who brings the peacocks to dance.

You are the thunderbolt that splits the mountain of sorrow.
You are the axe that cuts the tree of suffering at its roots.
You are the great Goddess.
You rule fate.
In time, you devour all.
You consume the universe.
You liberate all from their debts of past action.
Your mercy inspires awe.
You calm the demons of lust and anger.
You are both perishable and imperishable.
You rule all worlds.
You support the universe.
You incite the play of ignorance, passion, and goodness.
You are all worldly blessing.
You see all that exists, throughout the worlds and within the mind.
You are the balance of nature that brings freedom.
You bestow the merits of heavenly birth.
You are pure.
You are like a flower petal, offered to the sacred fire of purification.
You are the power of desire turned inward.
You are the torchbearer of spirituality.
You are a living sacrifice.
You adore vows of any kind, be they those of marriage
or renunciation.
You are worshipped, day and night.
You respond to the cry of surrender.
You are easily pleased by offerings of trumpet flowers,
from which you sip sweet nectar.
Your greatness cannot be fathomed by mind.
You live on the mountain that is home to the gods.
You adore the blossoms of the coral tree.
You are the beloved of heroes.
You are the power of the universe.
You are steadfast.
You look outward in all directions.

You are the innermost essence.
You are the ever-present space.
You give life to all.
You are the breath.
The sun rises to light the world you create.
Your mind is absorbed by the chanting of *mantra.*
You harmonize the realms of body, mind, and spirit.
Your army brings everlasting peace.
You are devoid of nature's passions.
You live within and beyond the natural world.
You are truth, bliss, and wisdom made manifest.
You are fond of the songs of truth.
Your limbs are holy.
You wear a garland of beauty and brilliance.
You fulfill all desire.
You are the essence of desire.
You are the ocean of inspiration.
You adore poetry.
You are the subtle beauty of the arts.
You are the wellspring of nectar.
You are well-nourished.
You are most ancient.
You are worshipped by all.
You are as fresh as the lotus blossom.
Your eyes dance with music.
You are the light behind all light, be it sun, moon, fire, or consciousness.
You are the sole refuge.
You are the space within the atom and beyond the universe.
You transcend the changing lights of dawn and dusk.
You hold the binding cord of worldly love.
You liberate all beings from worldly bondage.
You break the spell of the world's enchantment.
You are the illusion of form.
You are formless.

You are contented amidst the changes of the universe.
You know ultimate truth in the impermanent world.
You are the true beloved.
You are noble truth.
You are the beauty of created being.
You are faithful to creation.
You bring creation to life.
You are the truth of creation.
You care for all beings.
You are of myriad forms.
You are worshipped by the wise who seek the truth of unity.
You create all, from earth to ether, and beyond.
You feign wrath to preserve righteousness.
Your law brings freedom.
You are the foundation of the world.
You experience all beings as yourself.
You rein in the senses as if they were wild horses.
You please the senses endlessly.
You are the eternal wreath of letters.
You are untainted by action.
You are ever holy.
You birth heroes.
You are the primordial ether.
You are the most precious jewel.
In you, bliss resides.
You are the taproot of life.
You are the wisdom of being.
You remedy the pain of birth and rebirth.
You spin the wheel of illusion.
You are the steady worship that yields wisdom.
You are the thread of wisdom.
You are the source of *mantra*.
Your waist is slender, like a graceful bridge from desire
to consciousness.
You are known to all.

Your glories are limitless.
You are the breath of the spoken word.
You lend solace to those near death.
You are praised throughout the Upanisads.
You are the essence of peace.
Your depths are endless.
You rest in space.
You raise each being as your child.
You sing with clear devotion.
You calm the crashing waves of the mind.
You are the supreme goal.
You are the end of all pain.
Your love is without beginning or end.
You are untouched by cause and effect.
You are the overflowing river of pleasure.
You wear shining golden earrings.
You take form only to play.
You are ever unborn.
You are free in form.
You infatuate all.
You are easily pleased.
You can be known by looking into the heart.
You elude those distracted by the world.
You are the source of the Vedas.
You are the past, present, and future.
You pervade time as the eternal *omkara.*
You rule the three cities of body, mind, and soul.
You are free of illness.
You depend on nothing and support all.
You delight in the bliss within.
You are the river that floods the world with bliss.
You rescue those who are caught in the current of illusion.
You adore sacrifice.
You perform all sacrifice.
You receive all sacrifice.

You support righteousness.
You are the treasure house of material and spiritual wealth.
You bestow gold and grain.
You are beloved to the wise.
You bring the sage to be reborn.
You turn the world.
You absorb the universe in the depths of your belly.
You are the fire of renunciation.
You are the eternal refuge.
You appear to uplift the world.
You are unborn.
You are the source of creation.
You stand strong in the face of ignorance.
You are the distant shore of freedom.
For you, heroes are victorious.
You are valour.
You are the peace that calms all strife.
You are the shimmer of cosmic sound.
You are the wisdom of the heart.
You are the elixir of light.
You are artful creation.
You rest in changeless being.
You are the essence of the elements.
You are the truth of the natural world.
You bring to life the *mahavakya*, "Thou art That."
You listen joyfully to Vedic chants.
You are as gentle as moonlight.
You are wedded to silence.
You are the subtle balance between effort and grace.
You light the path like a delicate lamp.
You are fiercely independent.
You are slow and sweet, like honey.
You reveal all to be one.
You revere those who have realized truth.

The wise offer their minds to you, as sweet rice is offered
into the sacrificial fire.
You are the nectar deep within the flower of consciousness.
You are sublime.
You are eternally pleased.
Your light is as soft and rosy as the dawn's.
You accept all that is thought, said, or done as sacred offering.
You face glows like the shining hollow of a conch shell.
You still the pendulum that swings from longing to despair.
Your love cannot be bought.
You revel in the blessings that pass between beings.
You receive all praise.
You are praised throughout the scriptures.
You are the workings of the mind.
You calm the emotional mind, so that wisdom shines forth.
You are the great empress.
Your every deed is a blessing to the world.
You are the mother of the universe.
You support all creation.
Your eyes are large and luminous.
You are impartial.
You are bold.
You are infinitely giving.
You are ever joyful.
Your mind contains all mind.
Your hair is the sky above.
You ride the chariot of light.
You wield the lightning bolt.
You are the Goddess to whom the wise offer their lives in sacrifice.
You are beloved to all who perform ritual and sacrifice.
You recline on a sofa of five gods, four who kneel to support me,
with whom you are in union.
Union with you is eternal.
Your love is sacred.

You wear a sparkling necklace strung from the emerald of earth,
the pearl of water, the ruby of fire, the diamond of air,
and the sapphire of ether.
You are worshipped five times over with sweet pudding,
flower petals, butter lamps, incense, and holy water.
You are eternally worshipped.
You rule eternity.
You bestow joy.
You are all that can be thought of.
You bring forth the wilderness.
You are the daughter of the mountain king.
You are all that is treasured.
You are righteousness.
You water seeds of righteousness in the heart.
You transcend heaven and earth.
You command the forces of nature.
You are both intimate and everywhere.
You are soothing.
You are vibrant, like the red bloom of the *bandhuka* flower.
You play like a child.
You delight in the workings of the universe.
You bring about the height of good fortune.
You bestow sweet blessings.
You are draped in silk.
Your love is ever fresh.
You are pleased when a husband worships his wife.
Your beauty shines throughout the world.
Your mind is pure.
You are deeply satisfied with whatever is offered.
You are the cause of intelligent life.
You are emptiness.
You are worshipped with ten *mudras*.
You are the benevolence of truth.
You are the supreme union of *jnana mudra*.
You dote upon those who seek wisdom.

You are all that is to be known, as well as the path
to that knowledge.
You uplift those who have fallen along the path.
You rule the lower, middle, and upper worlds.
You balance the forces of nature.
You are the gentle Mother.
You are the triangle of creation.
You know no pain in the created worlds.
You protect creation fearlessly.
You spoil all seekers with the wealth of love.
You can be known easily through discipline.
You are all that is worshipped.
You overflow with compassion.
You dispel the shadows of suffering.
You can be known by all.
Intimacy with you humbles the seeker.
You dwell at the center.
You are the blessed Mother who rules in beauty.
You are absolute bliss.
You are eternal union.
You are the light in all.

May all beings surrender to you, again and again.

Acknowledgements

Verse 1 is reprinted from *The Dhammapada*, translated by Eknath Easwaran, founder of the Blue Mountain Center of Meditation, copyright 1985, 2007; reprinted by permission of Nilgiri Press, P. O. Box 256, Tomales, CA 94971, www.easwaran.org.

"A Babbling Child" is reprinted from *The Essential Rumi*, translations by Coleman Barks (Harper San Francisco, 1995), p. 94.

"The Vintage Man" is reprinted from the Penguin publication *The Gift: Poems by Hafiz*, copyright 1999 Daniel Ladinsky and used with his permission.

"Stop Being So Religious" is reprinted from the Penguin publication *The Gift: Poems by Hafiz*, copyright 1999 Daniel Ladinsky and used with his permission.

There is no end,
for there is no beginning.